# THE ULTIMATE PRIMER
## FOR THE
## SOUTHERN OUTDOORSMAN

# THE ULTIMATE PRIMER

## FOR THE SOUTHERN OUTDOORSMAN

**GARRY BOWERS**

SHOTWELL

COLUMBIA · So. Car.

Est. 2015

PUBLISHING

Produced in the Republic of South Carolina by

**SHOTWELL PUBLISHING LLC**

Post Office Box 2592

Columbia, So. Carolina 29202

**www.ShotwellPublishing.com**


Cover Design: Boo Jackson

Cover and illustrations generated using AI.


ISBN 978-1-963506-35-8

FIRST EDITION

10 9 8 7 6 5 4 3 2 1

# CONTENTS

# INTRODUCTION

This book isn't for everyone. It is not for people who live in big city high rise apartments, self-imprisoned in a sea of concrete and asphalt. Their idea of a good time is frequenting over-priced coffee shops and restaurants where a coat and tie are required. They live in fear they will mispronounce an item on a French menu. It is not for the politically correct, who wish to outlaw guns and sport fishing and attend rallies to showcase their ignorance. It is not for people who are so enamored with the nuances of identity politics, social equity and self-absorption that they cannot even laugh anymore. At anything.

This book is for the disciples of Isaac Walton and the fans of Henry Rifles. It is for those who salivate when they get a whiff of good camp stew. If you have ever found yourself calf-deep in Mississippi River mud, frozen half to death in a predawn Carolina deer stand or lost in a south Georgia swamp, you will enjoy this book. Participation in our sports allows us to appreciate and understand not only the natural world, but our own human nature. And it allows us to laugh. Even at ourselves.

Enjoy!

# 01.

# FISHIN' AND FEMALES

My lifelong friend and fishing buddy Ducky Jones and I were on his patio a couple of weeks ago enjoying some adult beverages. As is the habit of outdoorsmen when imbibing, our conversation turned toward the inane. We were creating names for groups of fishermen. We had just come up with a "cast" of bass anglers and a "dangle" of cane-polers, which, under the circumstances, were hilarious to us, when Ducky's wife appeared, with her own beverage. When Ducky saw her approaching, continuing our game, he whispered, "A backlash of ex-wives" and we giggled.

Now, Ducky has had more wives than Clint Eastwood has had gunfights. Consequently, I address all of them as "Darlin" so as not to call one by the wrong name. This day, I said, "Hello Darlin" and inexplicably added, "Nice to see you," before I realized the spirits of both Tennessee whiskey and Conway Twitty had invaded my psyche. I stopped before I added, "It's been a long time." Thank God I live in the Deep South. In California, a man can't call a woman "darlin" because they have declared that condescending and sexist. Pretty soon, nobody on the West Coast will be allowed to speak for fear of offending someone or being sued for sexual harassment.

Anyway, she asked, in a Southern Belle drawl simply dripping with magnolias and honey, what we were talking about. Ducky and I said simultaneously, "Fishin." "Of co-us you ah," she replied. I could listen to her talk all day. A native Southern girl can tell you to go to the devil in such a way that you look forward to the trip. She continued, "Y'all know, I jest looooove t' fish."

At this, Ducky snorted. "Yeah, she just loves to fish. As long as she doesn't have to touch live bait, tie on a lure, cast more than three feet, land a fish or unhook it. It's like someone who says they love to play football, but won't put on a uniform, run, block, tackle or touch the ball." Needless to say, Darlin' took umbrage with that statement, said, "Humph!" and departed the veranda, julep in hand, probably to retire to the drawing room of the big house.

You begin to see why Ducky has had so many wives. It has been worse. One of his "early" ones did not fish, did not like to fish and did not like Ducky to fish. And I don't think she liked Ducky. Those facts were no hindrance to his judgment, however. On their first Valentine's Day, he asked me what I thought would be an appropriate gift for Mary (Maria? Marie?) and I told him to get her some jewelry. He bought two matching in-line spinner baits, crimped the barbs on the treble hooks and presented them to her as a set of pierced earrings. She didn't like them much.

Her birthday rolled around and again he came to me for advice. I told him to get Marion (Maryanne? Marilyn?) something real expensive. He bought her a $450 bait casting reel. She threw it at him. Christmas came and for some reason, he solicited my advice yet again. I could see a pattern developing, so l emphasized he should buy Marilee (Marley? Martha?) something nice for the house. He got a topographical map of his favorite lake, had it enlarged and framed, suitable for hanging, which, incidentally, she tried to do to him. He did not have to buy her anymore gifts as she was gone by New Years.

My wife loves to fish too, and though she is a lot like Darlin' in the skill category, I never complain. She was the head chef at a seafood restaurant for years and she can clean a bass and cook a gourmet meal with it before I can find the fillet knife. So, I overlook the fact that only she and a six-year-old can manage to get their line tied in a square knot around the middle eye of the rod just removing it from the truck. Or the fact that she can never remember to put the stopper back in the cricket cage. "Look at all the crickets on the ground honey. Why do we have to buy them when you can just pick them up here around your feet?"

But my situation too has been worse. Many years ago, I had a girlfriend who had never fished a day in her life. Of course, she noticed that I lived and breathed bass fishing and wanted to participate. I taught her how to cast in the backyard with a Zebco and a practice plug. I regaled her with tales of my bass fishing prowess and patiently explained that even with my experience, the biggest bass I had ever caught only weighed 8 pounds, so she should not expect any miracles her first time out.

We went to a local farm pond one day and I tied on a spinnerbait for her because it required no presentation skills. Just cast it out and reel it in. Five minutes later she hung, played and somehow landed a bass I immediately knew exceeded 10 pounds. She was beaming and jumping up and down. "How big is it? How big is it?" she squealed. I frowned thoughtfully and hefted it up and down a little. "About 3 pounds," I mused and quickly released it. I broke up with her the next day. I know, I know, I'm going to hell.

Another very temporary girlfriend I had went to a small private lake with me one Summer afternoon. In the course of 15 minutes, she slammed the car trunk on a $200 worm rod, flipped the latch on the tackle box and then picked it up and then literally threw her rod and reel out into the water on an overhead cast. And she never quit smiling. She then went and got out a blanket and a box of fried chicken. She said, "It's so secluded out here, why don't we have a little picnic and then get romantic?" I told her I had a headache and took her home.

Now, before some wild-eyed feminist starts screeching like a cat caught in a woodchipper about male chauvinism and starts organizing boycotts and protest marches, let me hastily add that there are myriads of women out there who can fish circles around me. They can tie an improved cinch knot in half the time I can. They can fish a baitcaster all day without a single bird's nest. And they can actually detect a strike on a Carolina rig. It's just that the women with whom Ducky and I have been involved have not always fit into our world of fishing.

And we love fishing. And we love our women. But it is quite impossible to reconcile the two. I am reminded of the time I took my adolescent grandson to the doctor so he could get a severe case of hemorrhoids treated. On the way, I grinned and asked what he would do if the doctor gave him one of those 2" suppositories. He said, "I guess I'll just have to close my eyes and swallow it." I guess we will too.

## 02.

# PICKING A PARTNER

**F**inding the right hunting and/or fishing partner is an extremely important and serious undertaking and can sometimes take years. Ideally, it should be someone with the same level of love for your chosen sport and of similar skill level, personality and disposition. After all, you will be sharing one of the most significant portions of your life with this individual. Generally speaking, you will want to stay away from escaped convicts, politicians and weather forecasters. It is pretty obvious why you would exclude the first two. You don't want the third because hunting and fishing success depends upon the decisions you and your partner make, and weather forecasters are wrong a majority of the time.

My favorite partner is Ducky Jones. (I would have chosen him for his name alone.) However, out of a desire for domestic tranquility, I tell my wife she is my best fishing buddy. I can't believe she falls for that. Since she won't touch a cricket or worm, can't get her line untangled or unhung, and will not unhook any species of fish, you would think she would notice my frustration at having to spend most of my fishing trip tending to those duties for her. But, she says "Thank you" after each little task I perform. On a good day of fishing, I can get 30 or 40 expressions of gratitude from her. Exhausting as it is, I defy any other husband to claim he receives so many verbal gratuities from his spouse. So, I suppose it all evens out. On the other hand, it has occurred to me that she knows exactly what she is doing and is playing me for the idiot most people know I am.......Nah.

Ducky has many times scared me so badly as to require a change of underwear. He has almost gotten me killed on more than one occasion. He has embarrassed me to the point a lesser man would have cried like a colicky infant. On the other hand, he has saved my life, talked us out of several well-deserved tickets and at least one arrest, and made me laugh until I lost my breath. And he has accompanied me on the most successful trips afield I have ever had. He also backs me up when I tell my wife she is my favorite fishing partner. "Yes ma'am. You are all he talks about when we go fishing. It's Linda this and Linda that. Makes me jealous!" Ducky is so cool.

He is not the only guy I have hunted or fished with of course. I have been with a lot of people, but they just didn't cut it. Their potential as a perfect partner can most easily be evaluated by their actions. For instance, a neighbor down the street asked me to go fishing with him after he showed me his new bass boat. It was a tricked out, fully loaded, powerful craft that cost more than my house. I thought, "This guy must be a great bass fisherman" and I jumped at the chance to go with him.

We headed out the very next weekend. Though it was extremely windy, he roared up the lake at terrifying speed, whipped into a cove, cut the engine, made two quick casts, said, "They're not biting here," cranked up and tore up the lake again. This went on for 30 minutes. I thought the waves were going to beat the fillings out of my teeth. Finally, I told him I had to go back to the landing because my ankle was broken.

Another time, a landowner invited me to his place to do some deer hunting. We walked back to a beautiful winter wheat field. It was some of the most prime deer hunting territory I had ever seen. We climbed into separate tree stands about 20 yards apart and settled down to wait and watch. I had never seen nor heard so much activity and noise from a single human being in my whole life. He has a ceaseless smoker's cough and squirmed around so much you would have thought a possum was loose in his pants.

And every ten minutes or so, he would yell at me, "Seen anything yet?" Needless to say, I hadn't. A one-eyed, totally deaf buck would not have come within 300 yards of us.

Yet again, I accepted an invitation to squirrel hunt with a nice enough fellow who said he knew a place that would guarantee us a limit of bushy tails. He was right. The place was full of squirrels. Within 30 minutes, we had shot five each. I was using a .410 and retrieved all of mine. He was using a 12-gauge auto with high brass shells. We found none of his. They had simply disintegrated. I don't think he was so much interested in hunting as watching small mammals explode.

I've been with some real losers. One was a rabid fan of ultralight gear. Wouldn't use anything else. I told him the private pond we were going to fish had some real lunkers in it and he might want to reconsider and switch to some stouter stuff. He scoffed at me. On his second cast, he hung a bass that promptly melted the gears in his little reel and broke his rod into three pieces before the line snapped. We had been there four minutes, and he was ready to go.

It has been worse. I woke up in the middle of the night once at a deer hunting club cabin with this guy sitting on a stool by my bunk, staring at me. I screamed, he screamed, and then I screamed again. With no explanation, he went back to bed. I laid awake the remainder of the night with my skinning knife in my hand. And I let this other guy talk me into a float fishing trip. He made it sound great. But the current was so strong, I was actually only able to make about ten casts the whole morning. And on the one strike I had, I set the hook too hard, flipped over my canoe and was immediately swept away. When they finally found me clinging to a limb, two miles downstream, he was still laughing. He said I was lucky. Sometimes it took three or four trips for that to happen.

You don't have to go through a lot of experiences like these, though, if you just talk to folks. Listen to what they say, and you can get a fundamental idea of not only of their potential compatibility, but their incompatibility. I met a guy once at a barbeque and we started talking about fishing. This is what he said: "I recently purchased a bait casting reel with magnets so sensitive; the manufacturer guarantees an extra 20 yards per cast. And I bought one of those speed rods with an extra flexible tip that will generate enough power for another 20 yards of distance. I got a weighted, aerodynamic lure that will cast an extra 15 yards. I loaded the reel with small diameter high tensile strength line that promises another 20 yards. And I watched a DVD on casting techniques that swears I can add another 30 yards to my casting distance. According to my calculations, adding these increases to my average distance, I should be able to cast over two hundred yards. You want to come fishing with me Saturday and watch me cast?" I told him I had to have all my teeth pulled that day.

Most of the time, it only takes a sentence or two to make up your mind about a potential partner. For instance, you should never, ever, ever go fishing or hunting with people who say things like:

"The magazine on my new deer rifle holds 32 rounds and I can empty it in less than 5 seconds."

"Success is not how many fish you have caught. It's how many beers you have had."

"I didn't actually see any deer yesterday, but I did get off a few sound shots."

"I can't get boat insurance anymore." "They tell me them bucks has got horns."

"I'll bring a few blasting caps in case they're not biting."

"They kept askin' me if I had my safetyon. What's a safetyon?"

"That's why I've got a 225 hp on this baby. Ain't no game warden alive gonna catch me."

"The smell of cordite gives me flashbacks." "I decided to go into the guiding business when I discovered I could conjure up fish."

"I always carry a handgun on fishing trips. The FBI has been watching me for months."

"I only go duck hunting if my horoscope says it's O.K.."

"Wait a second. I've got to go back and get my huntin' whiskey."

"Don't worry about it. Those "No Trespassing" signs have been up there for years."

"When they're bedding, I like to bass fish with a .22"

"I can't go deer hunting this weekend. The spotlight on my pickup is busted."

"My favorite live baits are cockroaches and leeches."

"I coon hunt for a living."

"I caught a 7-pound bluegill last week."

"I've been thinking about joining PETA."

And above all, if someone asks you to go "noodling," run away. Fast and far.

I hope these tips will help you find a partner as good as Ducky Jones or (in case she reads this) my wife Linda.

## 03.

# GAME WARDENS
# AND OTHER SCARY PEOPLE

I know they are just doing their jobs, and I have never been treated unfairly by them, but game wardens, wildlife conservation officers, marine police, etc. are frightening. For one thing, they never smile. Not long ago, one walked up to me on a pier at a public landing and asked me for my fishing license. I pulled out my wallet, flipped it open with one hand, held it up close to my mouth and said, "Beam me up, Scotty." Nothing. I said, "C'mon, that's at least worth a grin." Nothing. Perhaps he had heard it before.

The inability (or choice) not to smile is not the worst thing in the world, I suppose. There are people who smile all the time and that's just as disconcerting. Lawyers and insurance salesmen for instance. And I've never seen an undertaker that wasn't grinning ear to ear. Now that's really scary.

Regular cops have a sense of humor. I was once stopped by a state trooper for doing 60 in a 55 zone and handed him my driver's license. Inadvertently stuck to the bottom of said license was a picture of my elderly grandmother mugging for the camera and making a really ugly Halloween face. The patrolman separated the two and his eyes got wide with feigned horror. He asked breathlessly, "What are you doing with a picture of my wife in your wallet!?!" After my heart started beating again, we both had a good laugh.

But game wardens are very serious people. I can't really blame them, though, especially during hunting season. If I had to make my living walking up on armed strangers, sometimes in a group, locked and loaded, in the middle of the wilderness, I might be a tad uptight myself. But they seem to be far too serious with fishermen too. It's like they expect us to drop into a ninja crouch and attack them with a worm rod.

Not long ago, while fishing a creek for bream, my friend Ducky Jones and I had an encounter he won't soon forget. Now, Ducky is a master at the backhanded compliment. "Man, that's the prettiest shotgun I've ever seen. I hope you can shoot it better than your old one." or "You can cast further than anyone I know. It's a shame you can't catch a keeper." That particular afternoon, after a game warden had obviously spent 30 minutes creeping up on us on his hands and knees through some low bushes, Ducky said, "Officer, you are good! We never even knew you were around. You must be the sneakiest, low-down unelected official in the state." Ducky laughed. The game warden didn't.

Unfortunately, Ducky had left his fishing license at home. He is the only person I have ever known to be arrested and jailed for fishing without a license. Imagine being put in a jail cell with murderers, rapists and robbers and you just know they are going to ask, "Whatcha in for?" The answer "no fishing license" is probably going to invoke both verbal and physical responses that will be, shall we say, unpleasant. So, in a way that only Ducky can do, he told them the truth. He said a state agency picked him up in a sting operation at a sporting event for which he did not have a permit. They all assumed he was a bookie and welcomed him as a fellow felon. He spent the better part of the night taking bets on an up-coming football game.

Personally, my most terrifying confrontation with the outdoor's finest occurred a few years back in the northern part of the state. I was camped out, fishing a small upland lake in the mountains and had not laid eyes on another person for days. A real wilderness setting. So, imagine my surprise when I pulled my little boat up onto the shore one afternoon and turned to find the biggest, ugliest, scruffiest game warden I had ever seen standing just a few feet behind me. I don't remember, but I may have screamed.

He was the approximate size of a small sasquatch. His XXXL shirt was way too tight. He just stared at me for a few moments. I initially thought he might be incapable of speech and would just start grunting and pointing. But finally, he said, "I'm gonna ast you a couple o' questions, boy, an' ya better not lie t' me" Still holding my chest, I panted, "You scared the bejabbers out of me, officer!" He replied, "I kin tell that by th' big ol' wet spot on th' front o' yore britches. Now, were ya fishin' and do ya have a license?" I answered, "Yessir" to both questions.

As fate would have it, my license, much like his ability to speak the Queen's English, had expired. He handed me a summons. "Ya need t' be in th' court o' Hiz Honor Justice o' th' Peace Jefferson Davis Turner next Chuesdy. This here's Satidy. That's tree days," he said, holding up four fingers. I started to tell him I appreciated the math lesson but thought better of it. Upon departing, he said over one of his very large shoulders, "An' don't lie t' him neither. They call him th' hangin' judge." I told him "Thank you" and added silently, "for not killing and eating me out here." No one would have ever known.

I showed up at the abandoned one room schoolhouse they called a court the following Chues...I mean Tuesday, pled guilty and Judge Turner fined me $100. Then he asked me if I had done anything else wrong while in his fine county. Remembering what the warden had told me about lying, I blurted out that I was camping without a permit. Another $100. He leaned forward, glared at me and snarled, "Anythin' else?" I told him I might be parked illegally out front. He said, "Son, you need to cut yore tongue out afore you end up in jail!" As I reached for my pocketknife, he told me to pay the clerk and get out. I did so forthwith.

There is one departure from my observations. Once, I did meet a game warden who smiled. A lot. My fiancée and I were fishing a farm pond when we spotted him walking toward us from the other end of the dam. We were fishing on the bottom for bluegill and my girlfriend had long since cast her redworms out and laid her rod down. He checked my license and then asked for hers. She said, "I'm not fishing, sir," at which time he unhooked a pair of mini binoculars from his belt, pointed to his car on a hill overlooking the pond and grinned like a Cheshire cat.

As he wrote out the ticket, I began trying to save her from a fine I knew I was going to have to pay. "It's her first time fishing," I whined. "It's not my first day on the job," he countered. I retorted, "I used to work for the Sheriff." He parried, "I still work for the governor." My final move: "I play golf with Judge Thomas." The warden beamed, "He's my uncle." Checkmate! He never stopped writing, and he never stopped smirking.

He was the exception. But as scary as they are, I'm glad they are out there. They stop some really scary people who are out to ruin our sport. The poachers, the illegal baiters, the idiots with the mental capacity of a turtle who fire at noises in the brush, a myriad of macho "catch 'em while you can—kill 'em while you can" common criminals, and the drunks who have killed so many brain cells they are incapable of rational thought.

Last year, the latter caused me such severe stress as to confound the rules of human physiology. It was late in the evening, and I was returning to the landing in my little 25 hp aluminum flatbottom, when an obviously inebriated Cretin in an 18-foot 225 horse v-hull almost ran slap over me. Such was my terror that body reacted violently and involuntarily. I bypassed #1 and #2 and went straight to #3. Don't ask.

Almost immediately, I got to watch the Marine Police officer pull him over. And I got to watch the handcuffs go on. And I got to watch him being carted off to jail. And the officer wasn't smiling. But I was.

## 04.

# NOTNUFF STEW

**D**ucky Jones has gotten quite a local reputation over the years among we outdoorsmen for a specialty dish he cooks on our camping trips. It is not called Notnuff stew because there is never a sufficient amount. On the contrary, there is always quite a lot left over. The name comes from Ducky's habit of sampling it during preparation, frowning, smacking his lips and saying "Notnuff salt" or "Notnuff onions" or "Notnuff taste," etc. The rest of us secretly refer to it as "Waytoomuch Stew."

We don't want to hurt his feelings, so when we go on these trips, we surreptitiously stuff our pockets with store-bought granola bars, muffins, peanut butter crackers and the like so as not to starve in the field. The basis of Ducky's concoction is O.K., even good. He brings with him three or four cans of chicken broth, salt, pepper and a large bottle or two of catsup. The latter is, and I cannot stress this enough, absolutely imperative. Catsup can make road killed armadillo edible.

Ducky's stock is fine, but then he supplements it with whatever game or fish we are after on that trip and whatever vegetation he can find. He claims his knowledge of various greens and nuts and roots came from his grandmother. I doubt that because if his ancestors actually ate some of the crap he puts in his stew, his family would have died out generations ago.

Now, I can understand the wild onions, dandelions and poke salad, but there are leafy green articles in there a trained botanist couldn't identify. And once, I found an acorn in said stew. "Ducky," I exclaimed. "Is this a hulled acorn?!?" "Yeah, why?" "Because they're poisoness, you idiot!" Everyone around the campfire immediately spit out their mouthful of Notnuff Stew. Ducky said, "No they're not! The acorn was a staple of the American Indian." I patiently explained, "Ducky, the American Indian boiled, dried and powdered them at least three times before they baked and ate them!" Ducky said, "Oh," then it was silent for a moment before he added, "Well, I boiled them once." Even Ducky had candy bars that night.

One pot of Notnuff Stew was especially memorable. You may find this hard to believe, but sometimes our group is not so successful in our quest for game. On one such outing, when we were hunting squirrel and rabbit, each of us returned to camp that evening, tired, dejected and meatless. Except for Jenkins. He reached into his game bag, produced a headless 5-foot rattlesnake and unceremoniously flopped it by the campfire.

Not realizing it had been decapitated by a load of number 6 shot at close range, I was 40 yards into the woods before the sound of hysterical laughter brought me to my senses. I slunk back into camp amid chuckles and chortles and an ensuing discussion of the merits, dangers and advisability of consuming a poisonous snake. After a lively debate, "Stinkin" Jenkins was the first to say he would be glad to give it a try. I didn't put much credibility in his decision because he works in a rendering plant where, among other things, they make glue out of cow hooves. And once, I saw him sitting on a dead heifer eating a souse meat sandwich.

But two others agreed. I remained conspicuously silent. That was no surprise to anyone. Given my well-known, life-long and extreme aversion to snakes, everyone knew I would be eating various wrapped goodies purchased earlier from the convenience store. After a couple of well-placed accusations leveled at the undecided voters ("Did your mother have any sons?" and "What color are your panties?"), everyone agreed on rattlesnake for supper. After all, we had catsup.

Ducky and Jenkins volunteered to clean the thing and prepare it for the stewpot. Neither had done it before but began the process with enthusiasm and a couple of sharp buck knives. I can't describe the process because I didn't look. To me, the sight of a dead snake is only slightly more tolerable than that of a live one. When they were finished, Jenkins proffered his hand to me with the rattles in his palm. I stared at him for a moment and said, "Did you take a course of Advanced Stupidity in school?" He grinned and stuck them in his pocket.

Ducky cut the thing up, put it in the kettle hanging over the fire, and began to stir it double-handed with a huge ladle he always used. I know it was my imagination, but in the deepening twilight, he looked like a medieval witch and a line from one of Shakespeare's sorceresses kept repeating in my head. "By the pricking of my thumbs, something wicked this way comes."

As prophecy would have it, sometimes around midnight after we had all turned in and I was quietly digesting my yum-yums and ho-hos, the entire camp was overcome with a case of flatulence the likes of which I have never smelled or heard before nor since. The sounds were deafening, and the odor was nauseatingly indescribable. Though it was quite cold, I drug my sleeping bag far from the fire and my fellow campers for peace and fresh air. Besides, it was a calm night and there was so much methane hanging in the air, I was afraid the entire camp might spontaneously combust.

Now, I don't know if this was caused by the rattlesnake or not. It may have been the extra helpings of Heinz products that were used, or it may have been some new wildweed that Ducky added to the pot. But I am convinced it would have been deadly to children and small domesticated animals.

The next morning, as we sat having coffee, grinning ear to ear, I asked the survivors if they were going to put rattlesnake in the Notnuff Stew again. There was a long silence and finally Jenkins spoke up. "I don't think you fully comprehend the detrimental effect that would have on hell's weather." I turned to Ducky and raised my eyebrows with the same unspoken question. Sport that he is, he thought a moment and replied, "Like the constipated fly said, ' I speck not.'"

# 05.

# A MEDICAL GUIDE FOR FISHERMEN

If most fishermen stopped and thought about the injuries they have had pursuing their sport and the high probability that those injuries would repeat themselves, they would all take up table tennis and there would be no books about the outdoors. So don't think about it. Just read.

Anyone who fishes is going to get stuck with a hook. This is the most common wound associated with our sport. The more you fish and/or the longer you live, the greater the likelihood of experiencing this painful event. As a lifelong fisherman and an old man, I have been hooked in all ten fingers at least once each, three toes, the back of my head, my right ear twice and once in my you guessed it.

Fortunately, the latter involved only a small wire crappie hook, and the crotch of my denim jeans were double stitched. It still drew blood. Hence, I was prompted to wear an athletic cup on all my subsequent fishing excursions. I know that sounds extreme, but when your you guessed it is involved, the peace of mind is priceless.

At some point, a hooking will be so severe as to require professional intervention. I have been to the ER so many times, the medical staff all know me. "Be with you in a minute Garry. There is a possible appendicitis in front of you. Coffee?"

Whether it is minor surgery or the attending shots that all physicians love, you need to be aware of their language and the interpretation thereof. "This won't hurt a bit" means you will have to bite your tongue to keep from screaming like a little girl. "This may sting a little" means you may break teeth clenching your jaws. If they say, "This might be uncomfortable," you should request to be tied to the table and gagged so as not to inflict reciprocal pain upon the good doctor.

I was once in an exam room having a treble hook removed from my middle finger. You know. The one you use to express dissatisfaction with medical personnel behind their back. It was embedded past the barb. It hurt. Yet the sawbones caring for me, obviously having graduated from the Marquis de Sade School of Medicine, decided I should have four (count 'em. Four.) local shots to help with the pain before he started digging. Each shot hurt worse than the original wound and each shot hurt worse than the shot before. Long story short, a wide-eyed nurse burst into the room claiming she thought someone was killing cats.

Accidental hook impalement certainly isn't the only injury we fishermen endure. There are lots and lots of wounds and impairments. Poison ivy, fire ant attacks, stone bruises, second degree sunburn, broken appendages, and accidental mosquito repellant inhalation, to name a few. When I was a kid, my Dad had a remedy for all of them: A good dose of castor oil. How that could possibly help a smashed finger, I never figured out. He was under the impression that the gastrointestinal tract controlled the rest of the body. I will say this. One tablespoon of that vile disgusting stuff would make you forget about any pain you were experiencing.

But I digress. In school, I majored in digression. And I minored in procrastination. Most all of the assignments I turned in were so off-topic as to be senseless, but at least they were late. And again, I digress.

A lot of our injuries are those the newspapers refer to as "freak accidents." One summer evening, I had an encounter with a very angry bat. He had attacked my top water plug and gotten hooked.

Stupidly, I was trying to extricate him. He bit me. So, I killed him. Before some screeching animal rights activist reads this and excoriates me on the internet for animal cruelty, let me explain so he or she will understand.

As I was in the middle of the humane act of trying to humanely unhook the bat and release it in a humane manner, it bit the crap out of me. It needed killing. Besides, I had to take its little squashed remains in to get it tested for rabies and infectious diseases. The tests were negative, and I didn't lose my finger, but it cost me an arm and a leg.

There are like 5 trillion kinds of insects in the world. Most of them bite or sting. And most of them live around water, which is one of my favorite places to fish. And I think most of them have assaulted me at one time or another. A majority of those occurrences were minor inconveniences. But they can be both agonizing and, like the bat incident, downright expensive. I was bass fishing from my 8-foot pram in a pond cove one Spring afternoon and got my spinnerbait hung on a small dead tree sticking about five feet out of the water.

On my first tentative yank to get my lure loose, the tree broke in half. It was as if hell itself had opened up and spewed forth the devil's minions. A tremendous swarm of huge red wasps erupted from that little tree and immediately attacked the nearest unfamiliar object: Me. Southern boys talk slow, but we think fast. In the wink of an eye, I abandoned ship. Even in the water, swimming for the opposite bank, I was the recipient of a dozen excruciating stings. Safely on the bank, I then faced another dilemma. That day, the wind gods, snickering and giggling, decided to blow my boat to the middle of the pond and let it slowly turn in circles. That wouldn't have been so bad, except said boat had a leak that required a good dipping out every 15 minutes or so with a plastic container I kept on board for that very purpose.

I sat on the bank, applying wet chewing tobacco to my wasp wounds (That was a trick from Dad that actually worked) and watched my little boat get lower and lower in the water. By the time I had gone through an entire pack of Red Man, the sun had slowly sunk in the west and my boat had slowly sunk to the bottom of the pond. With all my gear on board.

The only thing I was able to salvage the next day was my paddle and, in one of the Good Lord's great cosmic jokes, the plastic container I used for bailing, both of which had inexplicably floated back to the landing. I hate wasps.

Another common danger with which we have to contend is the snake. Now, there are several ways I am positive I am not going to die. I know I am not going to freeze to death on Mt. Everest. I am not going to be trampled to death at a Lady Gaga concert. And am not going to be eaten by cannibals in the jungles of Borneo. But I can't be sure about snake encounters. Those that won't hurt you will make you hurt yourself. It is a good thing my family does not have a history of coronary problems, or I would have long since been dead. I have stepped on them, sat on them, lain down on them and even inadvertently picked them up. I have never been bitten, but in each circumstance, I have been injured.

In the ensuing aftermath of these experiences, I have severely strained a groin muscle performing an Olympic broad jump; I have gotten a concussion running into a tree I would have seen under ordinary circumstances; I have dislocated my shoulder slinging a moccasin-wrapped stringer of bream across a pond. Once, I even shrieked so loud, I lost my ability to speak for two days. Wasps are not the only thing I hate.

Fishing is a dangerous sport. Be careful out there. And just in case, you should always have a bottle of castor oil on hand.

## 06.

# DUCKY JONES AND
# THE GREAT YANKEE INVASION

My fishing buddy Ducky Jones has a theory that most normal people would find, well, abnormal. He believes there is an organized, colossal conspiracy amongst our Northern neighbors to slowly and surreptitiously encroach upon the South and take over all of our fabulous fishing holes.

I have tried to convince him that no such scheme exists, to no avail. To fully understand the difficulty involved in trying to talk sense to Ducky, consider this. He once told me in all sincerity that if a bat lands on your head, it will get tangled up in your hair, lay eggs in your ears, and you'll go crazy. I asked, "How many have landed on your head?" He replied, "What do you mean?" I rest my case.

Ducky is a strange and unusual person. He is an acquired taste, like real cheap wine. And if you overindulge in his company, you'll get a headache. But I've got to hand it to him. He has an exceptional knack for sniffing out the Yankees he so fears. We were at our favorite watering hole a few weeks back when a stranger took a seat on the bar stool right next to us.

The guy says, "I was asking around and was told you two fellows know as much about fishing as anyone here. (There were only 5 people in the whole place) I was wondering if you might tell me where I might find a good fishing spot or two." Ducky looked at him askance and said, "Who wants to know?" His tone was such that had we been in a Western saloon, the piano player would have stopped and taken cover behind his bench.

The fellow told us his name and said that he was originally from here but had been in the Air Force for 30 years and had just retired and was moving back home. Ducky said suspiciously, "You don't sound like you're from the South." The fellow chuckled and told him he had probably lost his accent traveling all over the world for half a lifetime.

Ducky was not convinced. He said, "Sing one verse from any Hank Williams song." Fellow asked, "Jr. or Sr.?" Ducky said, "O.K., How many races did Dale Earnhardt win?" Fellow repeated, "Jr. or Sr.?" Ducky asked, "O.K., in what state was Ulysses S. Grant born?" Fellow said, "I have no idea." Ducky stuck out his hand and said, "Welcome home, son!"

Most Yankee accents are easy to recognize, and Ducky avoids people with certain dialects like they were afflicted with rabies. For instance, some are born with the inability to use the letter "R" correctly. They omit that letter in words that contain that letter: Noo Yawk and Noo Joisey. And they add it to words that do not contain it: Ameriker and Cuber. But sometimes they sneak up on him.

I believe I have told you that my wife is a card-carrying, certified, Italian, Cleveland Yankee. But she has lost most of her accent over the years and the only remaining clue to her origins is that she speaks about 40 decibels over the required volume for normal conversation. And Ducky is used to her. Consequently, he was caught off guard once when her cousin came to visit.

Ducky walked into the den one afternoon and I said, "I want you to meet Cousin Guido. (The mere name alone was enough to make Ducky's nose twitch) He wants us to take him fishing." Ducky asked, "What kind of fishing do you like to do, Guido?" He answered, "Da kind wheah ya putcha bait awn da hook, trow it in da watah, and have some beahs." Ducky walked out] I wanted to follow, but it was my house.

Ducky is really adamant about keeping Yankee fishermen out of the South. He defines a Yankee as anyone living north of Nashville and west of Texas. Hence, when his wife once invited her California parents to vacation with them so Ducky could take her father fishing, he became apoplectic. I don't recall her name but remember her because he said her mouth was so big, she could win a bobbing for grapefruit contest.

In near panic, he got on the phone, called California, and told her father he couldn't come fishing here because a 7-day out-of-state license cost $2,000. He was surprised when her father said that sounded reasonable. Then he remembered a 600 square foot house in Sacramento went for $1.2 million. So, he took the only alternative available. He divorced his wife.

Sometimes, Ducky's plans go awry. He and I had been fishing Lake Eufaula one summer morning and had quit about noon, pulled out our boat at the marina landing and were having a cold soft drink before heading back, when a Mercedes with a Connecticut license plate pulled up. A fellow with a fly-fishing vest and pressed Cabela trousers got out, walked up to us and inquired where he might catch some of "dose big breams" around here.

Without hesitation and without cracking a smile, Ducky pointed to a stump sticking up out of the water about a hundred yards from the end of the pier and told him, "We catch them right out there." He told the guy to go into the marina and buy a cane pole and a box of redworms, and he could rent a john boat and a paddle. Ducky and I settled onto one of the dock benches, sipped our drinks and waited. Sure enough, the guy emerged from the store with his new gear, got into an aluminum boat tethered to a slip and started out.

As he passed us, he said "Tanks" and I glanced around for a squadron of Abrams A-1's before I realized he was just being grateful for the advice. We giggled as he fought a 10-mph headwind and finally arrived at said stump. He tied up to it and commenced pulling in one two pound shellcracker after another. We watched in awe for about ten minutes. Ducky said, "I think I have one of my deer rifles in the trunk." I got him out of there.

Ducky's theory about the Yankee invasion may or may not be true. But he's not crazy. He has never claimed to have been abducted by aliens or to be personally acquainted with the shooter on the grassy knoll or suggest he knows how to catch crappie in August. He's just eccentric. And I'm lucky enough to have a friend who likes my Yankee wife. Speaking of which, I hope she doesn't read that comment about her being loud. She might get mad and yell at me. But I probably wouldn't notice anyway.

# 07.

# HISSSS

have had a lifetime of unfortunate incidents involving snakes. This has prompted me to finally form an organization called HISSSS, Hypersensitive Individuals and Sportsmen Scared Silly of Snakes. Our mission is multi-faceted, including the consumption of large amounts of alcoholic beverages at our meetings, but primarily it allows people to share their stories and fears with others who will not mock and ridicule. Instead of guffaws and snickers, we are met with nods of compassion and reassuring shoulder pats. It is, in effect, a therapy group, but not of the new age variety. Group hugs are not encouraged unless one of the female members are present.

There are people who are not eligible for membership. For instance, coon hunters are not welcome. Folks who walk around swamps, at night, looking up, just to hear a bunch of dogs bark, are certifiably insane. Ditto for herpetologists and zoologists. They actually handle the things. And rock stars who drape themselves with pythons need not apply. Also, people who attend "rattlesnake rodeos."

And there are specific individuals who have been pre-banned from our club, should they ever even consider association with us. Fred, a charter member, was on a dove hunting outing with his ex-friend Rufus and a half-dozen other men last fall. They were standing around together, preparing to step into the field, when

Fred emptied the entire contents of his 12-gauge auto into a crooked stick at the edge of the group.

Needless to say, most everyone was somewhat startled (one guy actually voided his bladder). For a silent awkward moment afterward, most just slowly backed away from Fred, eyeing him suspiciously. Someone finally said, "Hell, Fred. What was that all about?" Fred, who has a speech impediment, grinned sheepishly and said, "I thought it wath a thnake." Rufus asked, "Did it go hith?" That was wrong on so many levels. Rufus cannot join our organization.

Our chapter of HISSSS has by-laws, regulations and a mission statement. The latter includes education of the public, but children in particular. For instance, we are determined to eradicate, within our school system, the silly notion of scientific nomenclatures such as genus, phylum, species in biology when dealing with snakes. They should be classified as follows: Big, little, dead and alive. Even poisonous and non-poisonous are useless descriptors. All four classifications are dangerous. Those that won't hurt you will make you hurt yourself.

Case in point. A recent recruit, who understandably wishes to remain anonymous, joined HISSSS after an incident involving one of the most common of the sinister reptiles—a garter snake. He was cleaning out his bass boat and inadvertently picked the thing up with a handful of rigged baitcasting rods and reels. In the ensuing struggle to escape the snake and extricate himself from said tackle, he became so ensnared in a menagerie of lines and hooks as to require an emergency room visit.

While his wife was driving him to the hospital, she inquired as to what that awful smell was. He admitted to her that at the time of the attack, there were only two options open to him, and as he did not want to go blind, he chose the alternative. Parenthetically, regarding the attending physician, I personally fail to see how an educated person, who has sworn an oath of compassion to his fellow man, could react in such a manner that he did. A medical professional should not become so unglued as to fall on his hands and knees on the ER floor in a fit of uncontrollable laughter. Our organization is petitioning to have his license revoked.

Not all of that profession are bad. We have one medical doctor who was invited to join our club last month. His conversation was overheard in the pro shop of the local golf course. The good doctor told the pro that he had seen a huge rattlesnake on number 17. The pro asked him why he did not kill it. The doctor replied, "Because I didn't have a ten-foot driver." Automatic membership.

We are a diverse group. Our most recent member sought us out and asked to join as a sort of religious conversion. He admitted that he had spent his outdoor life purposefully scaring his companions and partners, most often using mankind's innate fear of snakes as the catalysts for his pranks. In his confession to us, he said he would sneak up behind a fellow camper around the fire when the conversation turned to snake stories, tap him on the back of the leg with a stick and then laugh with glee when the guy did an 8-foot broad jump from a sitting position.

He would lead a group of hunters down a deer trail on the way back from the stands, suddenly scream and take an exaggerated jump off the path and just die laughing when the line of hunters behind him did the same. By his own admission, he had been a sadistic, sick individual. But he had an epiphany.

One fine September afternoon, walking to a dove field with his companions, he almost stepped on a huge diamondback, expertly stuffed by a master taxidermist, and placed there by his friends. Since they never loaded their guns until they reached the hunting site, he promptly began clicking off shots from his empty pump, all the while yelling, "Snattlerake! Rakklesnate! Snakklerat!" Of course, they videotaped the entire incident and posted it on the internet. Instant conversion.

Had it not been for their raucous laughter, he admitted, he swears he would still have been immobilized on that spot, pumping and dry firing his shotgun and spouting nonsense until he grew old and died. HISSSS accepted him with the admonition, "Go, and sin no more."

I invite you, dear reader, to begin your own chapter of HISSSS. I would be happy to provide you with further information but cannot do so at this time as I have to prepare for tonight's meeting where we will be discussing the finer points of portable defibrillators. Good luck and keep your eyes on the ground.

# 08.

# ANGLERESE

The language spoken by fishermen is often complicated and difficult to interpret, especially for the uninitiated. We have a reputation for lying that is not always just. I have compiled a list of situational conversations with clarifications for each. Sometimes, the truth is "almost there" if one understands the nuances.

"Man, that is a whopper! You sure are lucky!"

"You don't need luck if you've got skill."

**Translation**: It was pure, unadulterated luck.

"How many bass did you catch today?"

"I didn't catch anything! I don't understand it. They were stacked up like cordwood and I threw everything in the tackle box at them, but didn't get a bite." **Translation**: I can't read my depth finder worth a damn. It might have been cordwood I was looking at.

After Joe went to his honeyhole, he went to his watering hole. He got stopped on the way home.

"What seems to be the problem, Occifer?"

"How much have you had to drink this evening, buddy?"

"Only two beers, sir." **Translation**: I lost count at eight.

"Wonder why we didn't catch anything today, Uncle Joe?"

"It's pretty obvious, son. The barometric pressure was rising, and the water level was dropping. When that happens during a full moon, they're just not going to bite." **Translation**: I don't have a clue.

"Any luck today?"

"I lost a monster! Snapped my ten lb. test like it was sewing thread!" **Translation**: I haven't changed my line in 6 years and was probably hung on a stump.

"You must have 50 bluegill there! How did you find a bed that big?"

"Years of experience. First, you have to know which side of the pond to look on. Then, wait 'til the wind is just right and you can actually smell them in a general vicinity. Finally, when the sun gets at just the right angle, you walk slowly down the bank, and you can see them plain as day." **Translation**: My nephew told me where it was.

"Dad, that was a huge bass! It's a shame you didn't land him!"

"Son, that was not only the biggest bass I've ever hooked, but the biggest bass I've ever seen. But you've got to be a man about it. You win some and you lose some." **Translation**: If you weren't here, I'd be sobbing like a schoolgirl.

"I've fished that delta swamp for years and not once have I gotten lost." **Translation**: I have, on several occasions, been bewildered for a few hours.

"I could have repaired it myself, but once you take the cowling off, the warranty is no good." **Translation**: I know absolutely nothing about outboard engines.

"I used to fish bass tournaments all the time. But I was losing that spiritual connection. You know, that feeling of man vs. nature. Competing against other fishermen for money and prizes sort of commercialized it and trivialized it for me." **Translation**: The closest I ever came to winning was a tie for 65th place.

"That's the reason Joe and I are leaving for the lake so early, honey. So, I can be back in time for your mother's birthday dinner." **Translation**: You'll be lucky to see me before midnight. And I'll have a buttload of excuses.

"I caught a 7 pounder today, but I released him." **Translation:** He jumped off right at the boat.

"It was terrible! I spent the whole weekend at the lake lodge with my fishing club and not a single one of us caught a fish!" **Translation:** We drank beer and played poker for two days.

"I prefer spincast reels for fishing plastic worms. The gear ratio is low, so I am forced to slow down the retrieve. I can cup the reel in my hand much more easily, allowing me to feather the line for casting accuracy. And of course, spincast reels are much more economical." **Translation:** I can just look at a baitcasting reel and it will spontaneously backlash.

"How did the fishing trip go?" "I got an 8 and two 6's." **Translation:** That's inches, not pounds. "How did you get all those bass tournament trophies, Uncle Joe?"

"Time and patience, my boy. Time and patience." **Translation:** It took me a lot of time and patience to save up the money to buy those trophies. "How many did you catch last weekend?" "You guys just kill me. You don't understand. Fishing has nothing to do with how many fish you catch. It's all about being outdoors, enjoying the scenery, breathing fresh air and relaxing." **Translation:** I didn't get a bite.

"My specialty is blackened bass." **Translation:** I burned supper again.

"Gee, that's an impressive string of lunkers you've got there. Where'd you catch 'em?"

"I'd tell you, but I'd have to kill you." **Translation:** I'd tell you, but I'd have to kill you.

## 09.

# FISHING FORECAST: CLEAR TO PARTLY BEFUDDLED

**M**ore than any other influence, weather affects the success of a fishing trip. With the possible exception of wives and hangovers. The weather determines when and where we go, our tactics and even the species we will seek. And more than any other source, we depend upon weather forecasters to tell us what the weather is going to be. All of them should go back to the college from which they received their meteorological degrees and demand their tuition back. Now, I have met several of them and they seem like nice folks and are quite intelligent. The fault may not be theirs, but their science.

Even with all the instruments, computers, gadgets and contraptions they have on hand, a medieval witch with a boiling cauldron of animal entrails could predict the future better than they do. They are wrong the majority of the time. Oh, they do pretty well in summer and winter when nothing much changes from day to day. But heck, I can predict the weather in those seasons. I can even make unimpeachable long-range forecasts for every state in the Deep South.

For instance, next August, it is going to be so swelteringly hot that you dare not walk to the mailbox without fear of spontaneously bursting into flames. Every day. And the only thing that will keep that from happening is the 99% humidity. And every other day, there will be a thunderstorm between 2:30 and 3:30 pm. After the storm and before sundown, there will be so much moisture steaming up from the ground that a catfish could survive on my front lawn.

In February of next year, the following sequences will take place: It will be sunny and freezing cold for three consecutive days, cloudy and warmer for three consecutive days, and then one night it will pour down rain and turn freezing cold again. Repeat. All month. If you don't believe me, cut this article out and read it again next year. It's not difficult, but they keep getting it wrong. And in spring and fall, worse than wrong.

Early one morning last March, I was watching the local weather to decide if I was going to go crappie fishing that day. The pretty lady on TV was pointing at a map and telling me that the chance of precipitation was negligible. I could hardly hear her for the rain pounding on my roof. Then, the screen went black because lightning had knocked the power out. C'mon.

For current weather, my wife can do better than that. She has a potted flower on the rail of our deck which she can observe from the kitchen window while she makes her morning coffee. She can tell me what's going on outside without stepping out the door. If the flowers are wet, it's rainy. If they are droopy, it's hot. If they are frozen, it's cold. If they are moving, it's windy. If the pot is gone, it's really windy. Foolproof. Why can't the weather people do that?

And I can personally predict whether or not it is going to rain on any given day all year long. When I was a lad, my Grandfather told me he could do that. He called it his "rheumatiz prediction." I silently scoffed at him. To pay me back for doubting Papa, the Good Lord saw fit to make me the butt of one of His great cosmic jokes, and I inherited Papa's rheumatoid arthritis. Before I get out of bed in the morning, I can flex my fingers and not only tell you if it's going to rain, but how much it's going to rain, to within one quarter of an inch. So, if you have a fishing trip planned and want to know if you're going to get wet, call up some old dude and ask him if anything hurts.

There are some fishermen who do not allow the weather to interfere with their plans and therefore have no interest in weather forecasters. My lifelong friend Ducky Jones is one such person. We had scheduled a bass fishing trip early one Saturday morning last year. I was awakened at 4:00 by horrendous thunder, looked out the window at the storm, shut off my alarm clock and went back to bed. At 5:30 there was a knock on my door.

Ducky stood on the porch dressed in a yellow rain slicker like the ones they wear on a tuna boat out of Gloucester. It was flapping about so violently; I assumed it was trying to beat him to death and escape. The rain was blowing horizontally, and he was having a hard time remaining upright. He squinted out from under the hood and yelled, over the howling wind, "You ready?" I stared at him for a moment, slowly closed the door without saying a word and went back to bed. I don't know how long he stood out there, but he was smart enough not to knock again.

On another occasion, he called me during lunch one day in the middle of July and asked if I wanted to go bream fishing. The sky was cloudless, there was not a leaf moving and the heat index was 110 degrees. A steelworker couldn't breathe outside. Roofers had quit work and gone home by 8:30. I said, "Are you nuts?!?" He said, "Why is everybody so interested in my mental health today?" I said, "Because you're bat crap crazy!" He said, "Awww, so it's a little warm. We'll fish deep." I told him I did not own a reel that held that much line and hung up. I'm sure he went by himself.

Fishermen like Ducky don't need reliable weather forecasts. The rest of us do. But we don't get them. A while back, my wife, out of curiosity, came into the den to see what all the raucous laughter was about. She thought I had come across an old "Roadrunner" cartoon on TV. I couldn't answer her query "What's so funny?" because I couldn't catch my breath. I just pointed to the Weather Channel. They were giving a 7-day forecast! 7 days! They can't tell you the weather 7 hours in advance.

It's not only their forecasting ineptitude; it's their complete lack of understanding of the sport of fishing. They will say, "It's going to be a beautiful day. Not a cloud in the sky." That's not a beautiful day for a fishermen. We like clouds. Lots of clouds. Then they will mention that the high will be 36 degrees. That's not beautiful either. They will occasionally give us the local lake levels but fail to note there will be a 40-mile per hour wind. It doesn't matter how much water is in the lake if you're going to get blown off of it. And they tell us the exact times of sunrise and sunset but not the times it will be light enough to see where you're casting or dark enough that you can't find your way back to the landing.

Somewhere in Houston, Texas, right now, there is a NASA nerd sitting at a computer controlling a robot on Mars. Mars, for Gosh sake! You would think they would convert some of that technology into viable weather forecasting programs for Mother Earth. I don't think they are interested. Now, I admire them for being able to use that equipment they do have. It takes me three tries to get to the word processor on my PC. If God had wanted me to operate a computer, he would have given me a brain. But I have sense enough to mistrust weather forecasters.

You've got to admit they are sneaky. Have you noticed they give you rain chances in percentages. Sounds like something a politician would do. Technically, they can never be wrong and ethically, we can't really gripe about it. Like I say, they seem like nice folks. But they smile all the time, like they are either drunk or hiding something. Sometimes I wonder if they are not just secretly laughing at us. It's not clear. At best, it's cloudy.

# 10.

# DAWGS

Outdoorsmen love dawgs. Before we go any further, we have to differentiate between dawgs and dogs. A dog is virtually any canine that science has declared is such due to certain physical attributes. A dawg is a dog that is a companion and co-worker for sportsmen, most notably hunters. Generally speaking, dawgs are strong, fearless, protective, loyal, trustworthy and helpful. Sort of like 4-legged Boy Scouts.

Dogs, on the other hand, are not. I tolerate them, but don't like them much. A great many of them are those little yipping ankle-biters who act like they just drank a pot of black coffee. They will bark at an intruder in the home, but you never know if the object of their annoying little yaps is a burglar or a roach. And a burglar can kick one of the animals across a living room. Can't do that to a dawg. Dogs are pretty much as useless as cats.

And I hate cats. To those readers who are feline lovers, I apologize to both of you, but I will not rescind my disgust of them. I think it may be because of the innate ancestral memory most of us have, by which we subconsciously recall our stone age forefathers clinging to the upper branches of a small tree while huge sabertooths circled below. Whatever the reason, I abhor the things.

Cats are arrogant, they won't obey you, they won't alert you to an intruder and they certainly won't attack one. And I defy any cat owner to challenge me to the cat-sniff test. I know if a cat lives in a house as soon as the front door is opened. When I was a kid,

I swept off the country church porch early every Sunday morning. One such day, an old deacon arrived and opened the doors. "Woooooo Wheeeee!" he said. "! think a cat done crept in, crapped and crept out!" He was so right. The building had to be aired out before services could begin. "Minions of the devil" come to mind.

And cats have gotten me into trouble. As we sat in the den one evening, two of my young granddaughters asked me to "start the fireplace." They watched intently as I built the fire, and I explained each step. One asked me what I would do if I didn't have any fat pine. I told her that when I ran out, I used kittens instead. I laughed, they burst into tears and my wife yelled at me. When I couldn't quit laughing, I then obediently went to my room as I was told. (A cat wouldn't have done that.)

Cats and dogs have some things in common. Neither of them can trail, tree, point or retrieve. Dawgs can. I will say this. There are a lot of dogs that are uglier than cats. Chinese pugs for instance. They were purposefully bred for centuries to look like that. Human beings can be cruel. The pug is an excellent example of why man should not mess in God's domain. There is no uglier mammal on earth. By comparison, the spiny anteater is cute. Besides that, I can't stand to be around them because they gasp and pant so much, I feel like they are sucking all the air out of the room, and I can't catch my breath. I have used duct tape to seal a leaky boat, hold a loose carburetor in place and repair a tear in a game vest, so it occurred to me I could wrap it around a pug's snout. But they don't have one.

Most hunters can't live without dawgs. They are not only our helpers, but our friends. And they are not always purebred labs, golden retrievers, beagles or blue ticks. Sometimes the best dawgs are of mixed ancestry. Many years ago, I had one that was a combination chow, husky and one of those Austrian breeds that I could never pronounce. He was beautiful, solid red and weighed about 80 pounds and I named him Tennessee (after the place they make my favorite bourbon). He was special not only because he could run deer with the best of them, but because it was with him that I realized dawgs could talk.

Most outdoorsmen know this, but few will admit it for obvious reasons. Granted, you have to know the individual, study expressions and understand body language, but it is no secret that they can and do converse. Tennessee used to climb the stairs to my deck each morning where I came out to have my coffee. One day, he looked around the corner post at me and said, "Hey boss, can I come up?" He sounded like the old cartoon character, Baby Huey. If you're not old enough to remember him, the closest I can come to describing his vocal tenor would be an articulate Scooby Do.

I would click my tongue, and he would trot over and smell my coffee cup. I assume he was checking to make sure I didn't have any whiskey in it that early in the morning. If I had, I am positive he would have scolded me. Then he would lay his head on my knee for his scratching. Tennessee loved me. I loved him back.

There are a thankfully small segment of hunters who do not believe in showing their dawgs any affection. I petted a pointer once as it stood in the bed of an acquaintance's pick-up truck. The owner came unglued. You would have thought I tried to set his animal on fire. "You cain't love on them dawgs! They won't hunt no more!" I asked, "If you kissed your wife, would she stop cooking?" He drove off in a huff. You can bet he didn't know his dawgs talked.

After having reread the previous paragraph, it occurs to me that if some feminist accidently reads this, she will become hysterical and start organizing protests for implying "a woman's place is in the kitchen." So please understand, madam, that I do not live in that magical fantasy world where absolutely anything can be interpreted as a slight to your "womanhood." I live in the real world where a huge majority of women cook for their husbands out of practicality. Generally, women cook better than men (except on the grill) and choose to do so willingly, probably out of self-preservation. So put up your lighter and your bra.

Just as there are guys that display no fondness for their dawgs, there are some that go overboard the other way. My friend Ducky Jones, like me, has owned dawgs most all of his life. He feeds his current animal steak once a day. And he's done that with every dawg he has ever had. Now, this is a guy who believes the five major food groups are boiled peanuts, chips, dip, slim jims and beer. He spends more grocery money on his dawg than on himself. Silly man. Oh, he eats beef too, but only the cheaper cuts, like liver and tongue. I asked him how he could choke that stuff down. He simply replied, "Catsup."

Ducky's dawg is named Spot. It occurred to me once that every dawg he has ever had was named Spot. I asked him why and he explained he didn't want to accidentally call his new dawg by the name he had for a previous dawg because "it might cause hurt feelings." Ducky is a strange and unusual guy. I don't tell him that though because he gave the pick of the last litter Spot had.

Ducky also pointed out to me a while back that all dawgs weren't used for hunting. He had one that fished. Ducky's prior Spot used to ride in the bow of his bass boat. In the Spring, he would ply the shallows with his trolling motor and when Spot saw a bass bed, she would bark twice and point. I swear I saw it with my own eyes once and alcohol was not involved.

That's not the last time I saw a fishing dawg. I was at a pond on my son's land a couple of years back and my grandson's dawg, Bullet, was following me as I walked the banks and fished for bass. I love the name Bullet. All real dawgs have great names. 'Ol Blue, Lightnin', Big Buck. That's another reason lap dogs and cats couldn't be used to hunt. Could you imagine, "Fetch, Fuzzy Boots!" Or, "Get 'em Mr. Puffy!"

Anyway, Bullet slowly waded into the clear water up to his chest and just stood there, very still, watching intently. Suddenly, his head darted under, and he came up with a bream in his mouth. He hopped up on the bank, dropped it in front of him and curiously studied it as it flopped around. I don't know who was more surprised, me, Bullet, or the bluegill. He looked up at me and said,

"Hey, did you see that?" I walked over and flipped the little fish back into the water with the toe of my shoe. Bullet looked up and said, "What the hell did you do that for?" I said, "You don't have a fishing license." He hung his head, said, "Oh," and walked off.

Here's something else. Have you noticed that canines can be broken down into two major categories? Floppy eared and pointy eared. Pointy eared dogs were bred for aggressive, combative roles. German Shepherds, Dobermans and Blue Heelers are war dogs, police dogs, herders and junk yard guards. A lot of them have bad attitudes and are even downright mean. Not so, floppy eared dawgs. They are friendly and caring and will sit patiently and listen to you. They don't have a clue what you are saying a lot of the time, but, unlike my wife, they at least pay attention and act interested. Don't tell her I said that. I guarantee she will listen then.

Here's something else you may not have noticed. People can be broken down into the pointy eared and floppy eared categories too. Floppy eared people include grandpas, ministers, and little old ladies at bake sales. Pointy eared people include most all politicians, irate cops on hot summer days, and slum lords. Oh yeah, one-eyed kindergarten teachers and fat, sweaty lunch line servers. I don't like pointy-eared people.

Anyway, I've got to go now. Spot just walked up, nudged my leg and said, "Hey Boss. It's almost suppertime." I've got to go thaw a steak. Damn Ducky Jones. I leave you with one last thought. A true outdoorsman cannot live without duct tape, catsup and dawgs.

# 11.

# GREAT MYSTERIES
# OF THE GREAT OUTDOORS

To explain mysterious phenomenon, we first have to determine the definition of the word. A mystery is not just something strange or unusual. For instance, my hunting and fishing buddy Ducky Jones has a rear-view mirror on his stationary bike. That is bizarre at first glance, but there is a perfectly logical explanation. Ducky is weird. Nothing mysterious there. He has been that way all his life. When we were kids on the local baseball team, he was the catcher. But he insisted on telling everyone that he played fourth base. Like I said, just weird.

Another example of something that initially seems mysterious are the policies of PETA. As you know, they want to outlaw sport hunting. When it was pointed out to them that, should they be successful, the impending burgeoning deer population would destroy all of our food crops, they had a simple solution. Government agency hunters would kill the excess deer. Whaaaat?!?!?!? Again, at first glance that seems like a mysterious response. It's not. They are completely bereft of common sense and incapable of rational thought. In other words, clinically insane. No mystery there.

And superstition should not be confused with mystery. I know a guy who is incapable of success on any hunting or fishing trip unless he is wearing his camouflage boxer shorts. Unless you are planning on frolicking around in the woodlands half-naked, there is no need for camo underwear. That activity should remain in the realm of elves and pixies. Superstition, much like PETA's logic, is a mental aberration, not a mystery.

Camo wallets, on the other hand, are a true mystery. Why on God's green (and leafy) earth would any outdoorsman carry a camouflage wallet. Think about that for a moment. The great outdoors are full of mysteries. Perhaps you have experienced some of these.

You cast your top water plug out and lay your rod and reel down and reach into your back pocket for a chew of tobacco. Boom! You get a strike. By the time you fumble around and pick the rod up, the fish is gone. I have done a long term statistical scientific study of this enigma and found that it happens 86.7% of the time. If you don't believe me, try it yourself. Of course, you can substitute the chewing tobacco with a handkerchief. Or a camouflage wallet.

Here's another. How come the drive to the lake takes a lot longer than the drive back from the lake? I think I may have a handle on this one. One of Einstein's theories postulates that the faster we go, the more time slows down. Of course, ol' Albert was talking about trillions of miles and the speed of light, and we are talking about a lake 20 miles away and a 55-mph speed limit, but I don't see why it couldn't be applied. If so, we need to slow down and we would get to our fishing hole faster. Perhaps, but it is still a mystery.

And another. Why does a bass strike a buzz bait? It neither looks nor swims like any fish, fowl, reptile, insect or mammal on this planet. What are they thinking? A fertile mind might imagine Daddy bass telling Mama bass, "I don't know what the hell that thing is Myrtle, but I think it's about to eat our babies! I'm gonna kill it!"

Here's a mystery that has plagued mankind since the invention of the fishing rod. Approximately 30 minutes before you have to end your fishing trip to go to an audit meeting with the IRS or to Easter Sunday church service or to a dinner date to meet your new fiancé's parents, the fish start biting like crazy. Never in your life have you seen such a feeding frenzy! What's up with that? This situation has been discussed around campfires and BBQ pits for time immemorial. I personally think it is proof positive that God has a warped sense of humor. But I could be wrong.

How come hot coffee out of a thermos tastes better in a deer stand than anywhere else on earth? It could be made from Louisiana chicory and burnt pine bark and still be better than any $8 cup in a gourmet restaurant. A conundrum for the ages. Speaking of beverages, when my son was a kid, it was a mystery to him why I preferred my whiskey from square bottles. I solved that particular question. I told him that round bottles roll out from under the seat when you put on brakes. (I probably should not have said that.)

How come all outdoorsmen love puppies? They are the only animal in the world that can change a full-grown manly man into a fawning idiot. I react to puppies the same way my wife reacts to babies. I say, "awwwwwww and rush to pick it up and cuddle it. I know that behavior is emasculating, but it has an upside. Whenever we keep our infant grandkids, I never have to change the diapers. My wife is afraid I'll rub their noses in it and put them out the door.

A discussion of mysteries would not be complete without bringing up mythical monsters. The only one we have in the Deep South is the Skunk Ape. It is a smaller version of Big Foot or Sasquatch. It is still very tall and hairy, but has red eyes, a blank expression and smells awful. Come to think of it, that is a perfect description of Ducky's second wife. Maybe after the divorce, she escaped into the wild.

I don't know if the Skunk Ape exists or not, but there is no mystery as to how I would react should I run across one while hunting. I would probably soil myself, accidently blow a hole in my foot, and frantically hobble blindly through the woods until I passed out. I hope to never see one.

Finally, here is a genuine mystery. I don't understand why otherwise perfectly sane folks would actually pay me to write this stuff. They must not know I would do it for free! But shhhhhh. That will be our little secret.

# 12.

# GOOD EXCUSES
# AND WHEN TO USE THEM

Perhaps the most overlooked skill an outdoorsman can have is the ability to make excuses. Especially if, like me, you are unsuccessful at hunting and fishing more often than not or if your sport interferes with your family or work obligations or if you just do something stupid. I am quite adept at the last one. "I forgot" is rarely an acceptable excuse. When the game warden growls, "Didn't you know there was a slot size limit on bass in this lake"? When your wife asks, "How could you spend the entire day fishing on our anniversary"? When your buddy exclaims, "You're not telling me you left the dock without filling up with gas"!?!

"I forgot" just doesn't cut it. You embarrass yourself and everyone around you. Before you use that the next time, consider this. What if an IRS agent asked you why you haven't paid your taxes for the last three years? In what conceivable universe would you reply, "I forgot?

One of my personal favorite excuses is "It was Ducky's fault." (Even that is a better answer for the IRS agent.) I blame my fishing and hunting buddy Ducky Jones for almost everything. And that's O.K. because he blames me too. It's sort of a Code of the Wilderness. And we always back each other up. If I'm late getting home, I tell my wife "Ducky got lost in the woods again and I had to go back in and get him." Or "Ducky's piece of crap pick-up broke down again." Or "Ducky told me it was only 4:00."

Of course, after all these years, "It was Ducky's fault" doesn't work very well on my wife because she's heard it hundreds of times. Her eyes sort of glaze over and she murmurs something purposefully unintelligible and probably obscene. But when Ducky tells his wife, "It was Garry's fault," she tends to believe him because she hasn't heard the excuse that often. That's because Ducky goes through wives like popcorn through a goose.

His current wife (or as I call her, his spouse du jour) always falls for it. I think he has had so many wives because he has given his last four a shotgun for their birthday. None of them hunted.

An acquaintance once told me, and I quote, "I kilt me two quails yestiddy and coulda got twict that but onliest had one box o' shells." If you overlook the complete destruction of the Queen's English, there is a perfectly viable excuse in there. Those "quails" are hard to hit. And if you are not using a dog and a covey breaks at your feet, it scares the bejabbers out of you. You never aim your first two shots and by your third, they are too far away to hit. "Lack of ammo" is an excellent excuse, and I have used it on more than one occasion.

Never, ever say things like, "They just weren't biting." That makes you look stupid and inept. For gosh sakes, blame it on the weather. It was too hot, too cold, too windy, too cloudy, etc. ad infinitum. "I think the temperature dropped too quickly" is a lot better than "They just weren't biting." The cajoling and ridicule will never end.

Have you ever seen a wounded raccoon fall on a guy's head and try to eat his face off? I have. It's not pretty. But that's what you'll feel like your friends are doing if you say, "They just weren't biting." "I was abducted by aliens" is a lot better than "They just weren't biting."

Sometimes you have to be quick with your excuse. Shoot from the hip. Another friend of mine (Yes, I have more than one) named Jake Jenkins pointed this one out to me. His nickname, by the way, is Stinkin' Jenkins because of his proclivity to make his own catfish bait. Jake loves to fish for cats. And each batch of bait he makes is more odiferous that the last. No amount of showering or scrubbing can get rid of the stench. It follows him around like Pigpen's dust cloud.

One day, at the rendering plant where he works, his boss said to him, "Jenkins, where were you yesterday? I heard you went on a fishing trip!" Jake replied, "Oh, no sir! You must have misunderstood. I went on a mission trip. You know, feeding the poor. That sort of thing. Perhaps you would like to come with us next time and join in the glory of giving?"

That was actually a brilliant statement because his boss would not allow any political or religious conversations in the workplace. Not only did Jake give an excuse for his absence, but he immediately ended the dialogue and any messy follow-up questions which might occur. I told Jake, though, that it was not an excuse he proffered, it was just a flat out lie. He disagreed, pointing out that he was poor, and the point of the trip was to give himself a good meal. Amen, brother!

Sometimes, if the situation is exceptionally dire, it is best to string a bunch of excuses together. The weekend before Thanksgiving, I straggled home on Sunday night, turkeyless. My wife stood in the kitchen, hands on her hips. It was a tirade. "Where's the bird? Huh? Remember what you told me before you left Friday? 'Don't go buy a turkey, honey. I'll be bringing one home.' Well, I took you at your word and now the grocery store will be sold out. What are we supposed to have for Thanksgiving?"

I replied, "It was awful. To start with, I forgot my lucky underwear. And you know I have no confidence without my lucky underwear. Then, we camped out in a field of goldenrod, and I spent two days sneezing. I must have scared every turkey out of the county. On the way back to the truck this afternoon, I spotted one and had it right in my sights when the frammerator fell off of my gun (Don't worry, she won't ask). But mostly, my mind just wasn't on hunting. I couldn't stop thinking about how much I missed you."

Her eyes softened. "Awwww, it's O.K. sweetheart. I'll just go buy a ham." If you had been there, it would have been at this point that I would have looked over my shoulder at you and winked. My wife is right. Men are such pigs.

Lastly, be creative. I have been asked more times than I care to remember, "How the hell did you miss that shot?" I've never given the same answer twice. "Obviously, the moon is in its apogee, which everyone knows changes the gravitational pull of the earth and therefore the direction of lead shot." Or "I thought I had my 20 gauge instead of this .410." Or "Cheap, reloaded shells!" Or "The afternoon sun was in my eyes" (Be sure you are facing west if you use this one.) And if all else fails, simply shrug and say, "It was Ducky's fault."

# 13.

# FORBIDDEN PLACES

**W**e outdoorsmen sometimes find ourselves in locales we should not be. This is sometimes caused by poor decisions, bad luck or blatant stupidity. Most of the hazardous situations I have found myself in have been directly attributable to the latter. My friend, Ducky Jones, however, experienced one of his most harrowing moments due to ignorance. The root word of "ignorance" is "ignore." Ducky is a master of ignorance.

In his younger days, when he was in the military, he was stationed in California, where a friend of a friend invited him to a fashionable soiree near Hollywood one weekend. Ducky chose not to hear the words "Actors Guild," "activist fundraising" or "elite society." He did hear the words "party," "booze" and "women," so he borrowed a suit and went. At said cocktail party, he ended up, free drink in hand, with a small group of gentlemen involved in a lively discussion of hobbies.

One said that almost every weekend, he joined a flotilla of yachts hell bent on saving the whales. Another bragged of his participation in organized protest marches to stop the logging of innocent trees. Still another told of his exploits to find a spotted desert salamander so he could have it placed on the endangered species list and stop all road construction on the west coast. One chap asked Ducky what he did in his spare time.

It was one of those great galactic coincidences that happen once in a lifetime. Everyone in the room simultaneously and inexplicably stopped talking at the precise moment Ducky replied, "I deer hunt." That short sentence echoed off the walls of the ballroom like it had been announced over a stadium speaker. There was an audible and collective intake of air and the unmistakable sound of a monocle falling into a martini glass. Everyone in the room was looking at him as if he had confessed that he burned babies alive.

In the deathly silence, some high-pitched anonymous voice cracked with saintly piety, "Why do you kill defenseless animals?" Ducky glanced at the formal buffet dining table, covered with pate', caviar, and gourmet roasts and the little devil on his shoulder made him say, "I just love to watch them die." The crowd gasped again. One lady fainted and another gagged.

The men in his group stepped back as if they had just discovered he had leprosy. Ducky drained the whiskey sour he was holding in one gulp and headed toward the door. The crowd parted like the Red Sea. Before someone produced a length of rope and threw it over one of the hand hewn Victorian rafters, Ducky departed the premises, found a tavern down the street with a sailfish over the bar, and finished his night of revelry.

We do not go to all forbidden places on purpose. A few years back, I got hopelessly lost in a sparsely populated part of a neighboring county looking for a wildlife management area on which to deer hunt in the upcoming season. I would say I drove in circles for several hours, but since I never passed the same place twice, it wasn't circles. I was in a maze of logging roads, old four-wheeler tracks and game trails that would have frustrated a lab rat. When I came across the only man-made structure I had seen all afternoon, I pulled up to the porch and was greeted by a shirtless man in overalls with a shotgun in the crook of his arm. I tentatively stepped out of my truck.

"Yew one o' 'em land manage-mint fellers?" he asked as he let loose a stream of tobacco juice at one of the dogs on the steps. "No sir," I managed to croak. "Well, ya caint be hyar t' court one o' my daughters. Th' oldest 'un ain't but 12. She won't be marryin' age til next yar." I glanced quickly at the girls that had gathered on the porch behind him. They all looked like female Howdy Doody puppets. "Oh, noooo sir," l said, wide-eyed. "Well, jest whut's yore problem, boy?"

"I'm lost sir." He squinted suspiciously. "Yew caint be lost. This hyar road yore on can ventually take ya t' New Yawk City." I thought about that for a moment. He was right. This pig trail would at some point turn into graded dirt into secondary pavement into county two lane into four lane into interstate and voila! New Yaw... York City, which, by the way, is another forbidden place, according to Hank Williams, Jr. "I'd rather go to hell than New York City, it's all the same to me." There's always a lot of truth in country music.

Anyway, he obviously felt pity for the stupid big city feller and said, pointing, "Ya go down nar about a mile, a good mile, an' take a hard rite. Then go til ya git t' whar th' ol' Johnson place burnt down about 10 yar ago." I wanted to ask him how I would see it since it had been nonexistent for a decade, but he was still holding a shotgun and seemed somewhat impatient with me. "When ya cross the crick, th' road'll fork. Take the muddiest 'un." I politely nodded as if I knew exactly what he was talking about, thanked him profusely, took my leave and wandered around for another two hours before I found my way out.

Sometimes you are deep into a forbidden place before you even realize it. Once I was fishing a sprawling lake when nature called. I pulled into a secluded feeder creek cove, looked carefully around and determined it was devoid of human life. After I got up on the bow of my bass boat and began to relieve myself, I discovered my original determination had been bad wrong. On a tiny pier, partially hidden by a willow tree, three little old ladies sat cane pole fishing. I heard the hysterical laughter before I actually saw them. I stopped in mid-stream, so to speak.

In my haste to extricate myself from the situation, I hung myself in my zipper. When I screeched like a little girl, the guffaws and knee slapping increased in both volume and intensity to the point I thought one of them might grab her chest and fall over dead. I could just see the headlines: "Local Fisherman Kills Elderly

Lady." I left that slough much more quickly than I entered. And I never looked back.

For an adult, forbidden places are bad enough, but for a kid, it's much worse. There were almost too many to count. And as a kid, you were required to go to them. When I was around ten, one of those places was a strip mine pond to which my mother had told me to never, ever go fishing. One day, I walked into the back door and Mom snatched me up and began wailing on me with a cherry tree switch. (If you have never experienced this particular form of punishment, you have no true appreciation of life.) Since I was wet, muddy and had a cricket cage tied to my belt, denial was out of the question.

Occasionally, the geographic location is not the forbidden place, but the conversation. Once, I walked into a back door whipping frenzy and screeched, "What did I doooooooo?" Keeping cadence with the licks, she replied, "You...know...very...well...what...you... did!" Actually, I didn't. But I wasn't about to confess anything, because it may have been an event she did not yet know about.

Another example of prohibited dialogue occurred just a few weeks ago. My wife and I were fishing a farm pond, and she called me over for the umpteenth time to say, "I'm hung." Frustrated with the constant interruptions, I replied snidely, "That's what I'm supposed to say." Her expression replied, "Don't even go there." Her expression continued, "I will make a complete fool out of you." Her expression added, "And possibly bring you to tears." It is amazing what a wife can say without opening her mouth. Some forbidden places are easy to recognize before you even get there.

# 14.

# DON'T YOU JUST HATE THAT?

Everyone despises Monday mornings, one irons, coaches who call a triple option to the short side of the field, February and souse meat. But after that, outdoorsmen pretty much have completely different dislikes than other folks. It's because our situations are different, plus we don't pay much attention to the mundane things other people find distracting.

For instance, non-outdoorsmen get upset when they have a bad hair day or when a Cyndi Lauper CD melts on their dashboard or when they spill gravy on their necktie. Outdoorsmen generally don't care much about their tresses or little metal records and don't wear neckties unless they absolutely have to. But we detest things other people are not likely to encounter.

For instance, you go to pick up a "dead" squirrel you just plinked out of an oak tree, and it sinks its little beaver teeth into that web of skin between your thumb and forefinger. Don't you just hate that? Or when you hang a monster bass on which you can barely gain line and while you're fighting it you're calculating the price of the taxidermist, and then it surfaces, and you discover it's a foul hooked carp. I really hate that.

It's early Spring and has been unseasonably warm and rained for three days. You wake up on Saturday morning and the sun is shining and visions of top-water bassing are dancing in your head. Then you walk outside and it's 26 degrees. Don't you just hate that? Or when you're out hunting and go to cross a fence you did not know was electrified. The saliva in your mouth crackles like pop-rocks, your eyeballs explode and your extremities go completely numb. And you smell burning flesh, but don't feel anything. At first. I just hate that.

Don't you just abhor those obnoxious motion activated singing bass mounted on the wall? There was one by the front door of a drinking establishment Ducky and I frequent. I made them take it down. Not that I am all that intimidating, but he and I are responsible for approximately one quarter of their annual revenue, so they were happy to comply.

Speaking of Ducky, he had a situation recently that he found particularly despicable. He was shopping at a Bass Pro Shop and wandered into the camping section where he stepped into an erected model wall tent, lay on the cot to check it out for size and went to sleep. He woke up at 2 a.m. On his way downstairs to figure a way out of the closed and empty store, he rounded a corner and literally ran into the security guard. They stood face to face and had a wide-eyed screeching contest for a few moments. Ducky said he really hated that. And the security guard hated it so bad he had to change his pants.

Because outdoorsmen are such rational people, we tend to loath illogical people. Now, when I was a kid, my grandfather used to take my cousin and I fishing, and he drove all out pedal to the floorboard wide open. It was scary. I asked him why he drove so fast, and he patiently explained. "Son, the road is a dangerous place with lots of accidents. The less time you spend on it, the less likely you are to have one." That was convoluted reasoning, but logical nonetheless.

I'm talking about people who have no logic at all, like the anti-2nd amendment politicians with armed bodyguards who want to take our guns away to "make society a safer place." I hate people who are so stupid they can't comprehend that the constitution gives us the right to bear arms to protect ourselves from government officials like him. I know, I know. We are supposed to hate the deed and not the person. But l have a hard time thinking in those terms. And I just hate that.

# 15.

# CHATTAHOOCHEE TALES

**S**everal years ago, Ducky and I took a trip to the upper reaches of Lake Eufaula to fish and camp for the weekend. It was in the boonies. It only took us two hours to get within sight of the Alabama-Georgia line but another two hours of interminable dirt roads to get to the commercial campground on the shore. The camping fee was exorbitant, really criminal, but they had figured out that no one was going to turn around and go back over those roads the same day they arrived. And we were there for the duration anyway when the proprietor pointed out that the juke joint across the road served Ducky's favorite beer: Ice cold. So, we paid, erected our pop-up tent, launched the boat and went fishing.

And what fishing it was! We caught and released at least 2 dozen largemouth, all on topwater. However, I caught the largest and that was unfortunate. If you are at all familiar with the Redneck Bible, you know that in the Book of Cletus, Chapter 4, Verse 2, it says "He who catcheth the biggest bass, buyeth the beer." And Ducky was thirsty.

Between the time we pulled the boat out and got it secured back at our assigned site, Ducky had said, "You know you beat me by a half-pound, right?" at least five times. So, as the sun set, we meandered across the road to a business that should have been listed in "The World's Most Forbidden Places." It was innocuous enough. The sign on the front read "Tiny's Bar and Grill by the Lake." I liked that. It was concise and informative. It gave you the name of the owner, the fact that they served food and drink and the location. Turns out, the only correct part was the location, which, come to think of it, was redundant in the first place since you already knew where you were.

When we walked inside, there were only a half dozen patrons, all shooting pool at the tables in the back. The bar stretched the entire length of the building. It was the biggest such structure I had ever seen in my life. The sign outside should have had BAR in huge, oversized letters. We walked up to one of the three waitresses behind said monstrosity, and I asked the young lady, "What you got for a couple of fat old ugly guys?" Without blinking, she replied, "Y'all ain't that old" and placed two canned brews in front of us.

She asked, "Tab?" and Ducky said, "I'd prefer a bottle." I said, "You buffoon, she wants to know if we want to start a tab." Ducky replied, "Of course, who caught the biggest fish?" I asked the young lady, "What's on the grill tonight?" and she flippantly pointed a thumb to the wall by the entrance door. There sat an old convenience store hot dog rotisserie with a couple of blackened, wrinkled wieners circling slowly on the spits. Beneath was a metal drawer which surely contained some rock-hard crusty buns. The GRILL on the outside sign should have been written in teeny lower-case letters.

We took our libations and sat down at a nearby table directly across from a small stage and an even smaller dance floor and listened to the "clicks" and "thunks" from the pool tables. This huge mountain of a man ambled up to our table and grinned down at us. I admired his dental work. His tooth fairly gleamed in his lower jaw. He said, "Hi, guys. I'm Tiny." Ducky said, "No, you're not." I cringed, ducked a little and said a quick prayer. But Tiny just chuckled and said, "I git that a lot." The TINY on the sign was the biggest misnomer of all.

His arms were formidably immense and something to behold. Each was bigger than both my thighs. His belly hung down to the point it almost obscured the obligatory oversized cowboy belt buckle. On the front of his stained shirt was printed "Security

Instructions," which seemed puzzling until he turned away for a moment to yell at one of the pool shooters and I saw' the back, which read, "Two in the Torso, One in the Head." He didn't open carry, but there were lots of places in his colossal rolls of fat for a hidden 14" revolver.

Tiny asked if we were from the campground across the road. Ducky, never at a loss for sarcasm, even in the face of death, said, "Yeah, but we would have driven two hours over rutted dirt roads just to get to this fine establishment." Tiny, thank the Good Lord, was obviously oblivious to sarcasm and replied, "Well, that's good to hyar. You boys enjoy yoreselves. Ifn thar's anythin I can do fer you, you let me know." And winked. For some reason, the theme song from "Deliverance" came into my head."

Before Ducky could say anything else to get us killed, or worse, I said, "We must have gotten lucky to get here tonight," and pointed to the sign over the tiny band stage in the corner that read, "This Weekend Only—Directly from New Orleans—Buddy Beaudrou and the Zydeco Three." Tiny said, "Oh, they play hyer ever weekend. That sign's been up thar fer years. They live in a wall tent on th' campground. Max gives 'em a special rate." I said, "Max? We paid a woman for our spot this morning." Tiny said sheepishly, "Yeah, Max likes to dress up sometime." I heard the banjo again. Before I could stop him, Ducky said, "That band must be reeeeeal good." Tiny looked somewhat surprised and replied, "Oh yeeeeeah, they are. Folks come from miles around to hyer 'em. This place'll be packed fore long." Tiny grinned again, proudly showing off his tooth and walked away. I said to Ducky, almost pleading, "Let's get out of here." He said, "You caught the biggest bass and I'm thirsty."

Tiny was right. About 30 minutes later, the rumble of unmuffled pickup trucks in the parking lot was almost deafening. People started coming in at a steady pace. Most looked as if they had come straight from work. They were in oily, dusty, greasy, dirty work clothes and generally disheveled. Then, the men started coming in. Where all these folks appeared from was a mystery. We had driven miles and miles and miles through wilderness with little sign of civilization to get here. But there they were, and they were a rowdy bunch.

The bar had no more room, and the pool tables were full, and I mostly heard, rather than saw through the crowd, an obvious loud loser at one table say, "Is that your wife over there?" The obvious winner yelled, "Yeah, what of it?" The antagonist replied, "Well she must be a great cook, cause she's too ugly to..." Wham! Well, that's not exactly the sound of the large end of a pool cue striking a skull, but you get the idea.

Then a couple of old women who should not have been dressed in leotards got into a fight over an old bald skinny guy, but it was pretty much over by the time their beehive wigs had been pulled off. Shortly thereafter, Tiny sauntered by our table and fairly shouted over the din, "Told ya. And th' band ain't even hyer yet." Even Ducky was ready to leave at that point. As we exited, I noticed someone had taken the burnt wieners from the spits on the warmer and became slightly nauseated at the very thought of it.

We laid in the tent and listened to the sounds of Cajun music, breaking glass and police sirens until three in the morning. Surprisingly, we only heard one gunshot. We got up about five and had another great day of fishing. By noon, Ducky had caught a four pounder, and I hung one I knew would tip the scales at six. I cranked my drag all the way down and she pulled off before I got her to the boat. At the end of the day, Ducky did not even mention "Tiny's Bar and Grill on the Lake." And just for kicks and grins, I'm not going to tell you exactly where it is. You can thank me later.

# 16.

# SPEAKING OF COMMUNICATION

Many things affect hunting success, including the weather, choice of guns and ammo, time of year, and whether or not your wife wants you to come home. But nothing is quite so important as the ability to communicate. When you mention "communication" these days, most folks immediately think of cell phones. However, the use of these devices most often deprive people of the non-verbal clues that make good transmission of ideas and information possible. With a cell phone, you cannot discern facial expression, voice tone or tenor, volume, body language, etc. and therefore you cannot perceive meaning. For instance, if you read "Kiss my big ol' butt" on a cell phone screen, you do not know if it is a threat, an insult, a joke or a romantic suggestion. In person, you know immediately.

To make things worse, it is popular nowadays to use shorthand on the insidious little things. "FYI," "OMG," "LOL," etc. For a while I thought the latter one meant "lots of luck," but became convinced it meant "lack of learning." And if you get into that teenaged valley girl jargon, it devolves into "LTFS" for "like totally fer shure," which would be an abbreviation for "Yes." Like, whatever, dude.

Hunters not only don't need cell phones; they have their own language and can communicate without a word being spoken. FI(for instance), you are in a deer blind with a buddy and a deer approaches from your assigned direction of observation. You go, "Psssst." Buddy slowly turns his head and looks at you. You turn your eyes to deer's location. Buddy does too but shrugs slightly and raises his eyebrows. You stick one finger from the hand resting on your knee, indicating 100 yards.

Buddy looks again and grins. He locks eyes with you and gives a slight nod, relating that you should take the shot. Suddenly, he makes a sound with his tongue and cheek like he's softly calling a dog. You cut your eyes to him, and he is holding his hand out flat. You hold fire. Buddy holds out two fingers. You look beyond and see a larger rack following. See how that works? Nary a word.

Now, I suppose you could do that on a cell phone. BAFM (Buck approaching from meadow) W?IDSB (Where? I don't see buck) OHYYD! (One hundred yards you dummy!) But this could just as easily be misinterpreted as BAFM (Back away from me) W?IDSB (Why? I don't smell bad) OHYYD! (Oh, hell yeah you do!)

Of course, if you are using wordless communication with your partner, it helps to be young enough to have all your faculties about you, like the ability to see and hear, two skills paramount in this endeavor. Ducky and I are aging and rapidly losing those assets. These days, we often fit one of his favorite axioms, "like the blind leading the deal." At first, that doesn't make much sense. But if you think about it a moment. Someone who can't see should not be giving directions to someone who can't hear. But remember, this comes from the fertile and inscrutable mind of Ducky Jones. Don't think about it too long.

We don't just communicate with people. We communicate with our quarry. (And you certainly can't do that with a cell phone.) If you are rattling antlers or blowing a duck call or tapping on a rubber plunger to tell squirrels to "come this way," you are, like Dr. Doolittle, talking to the animals. And they talk back. When you hear a deer blow, they are saying "I see you, numbskull, but you don't see me, or I would have been long gone by now." And when a dove is almost in range, but suddenly takes a hard, sweeping turn, it is saying "You should have worn camo, you idiot." (Game animals tend to call hunters lots of derogatory names.)

When we are transferring information with our fellow man, lack of specificity in our verbal language can be downright dangerous. For instance, when I was helping Ducky reload shotgun shells in his shop one afternoon last year, not having participated in that activity for many years prior, I showed him how much powder I had put in a twelve-gauge hull, completely ignoring the measuring implements and scales scattered around. He glanced across the bench and said, "A little more."

You wouldn't think a tiny word like "little" could be misinterpreted so badly, unless you consider the difference in a little jalapeno and a little catsup. We didn't. On our next skeet shoot a couple of weeks later, the chamber of his Mossberg inexplicably let loose with a deafening crack that caused some of the military veterans on the range to yell "Incoming!" and hit the dirt. As I have told you before, Ducky is one of the luckiest people on earth. Not only was no one was injured, but he immediately remembered I had "helped" him reload those shells. I had to buy him a new shotgun. And a new pair of trousers.

There is another set of words I have personally always had trouble with. As a hunter, "early" means 5 am (going) and 5 pm (returning). To my wife, "early is between 9 am and noon. That word has caused some, shall we say, misunderstandings between us. Even worse, for me "late" means we are going to stop at a bar on the way back. The only time my wife uses late is if it is preceded by the phrase, "Don't you dare be."

After his escape attempt, "Cool Hand Luke" was admonished by the prison warden, "What we have here is a failure to communicate." Subsequently, Luke was thrown into the hot box for several days. For those of you who may not know, that was an unventilated structure the size of an outhouse sitting in the deep south heat and humidity. My wife's punishment for my failure to communicate may not be a hot box, but it may certainly be construed as hot water.

Our English language is heavily burdened with words, most descriptive adjectives and adverbs, that have totally diverse definitions according to one's individual experiences. Light, cold, fast, ugly, good, stupid, funny, slow, heavy, hard, etc. etc. and on and on, a misinterpretation of any of these words can cause everything from severe trauma to family violence to terminal embarrassment. Speaking of the latter, take the simple word "red." Synonyms include crimson, maroon, ruby, cardinal, cherry, wine, coral, etc. My face has been all of those colors, depending upon which shameful situation had befallen me upon which occasion.

Like the time my *tang got all tonguled* up and I told my hunting buddies I was late because I couldn't get my car crunk. Or the time I was caught at the deer camp with a sock puppet on each hand carrying on a three-way conversation with myself. Or the time...never mind. Suffice to say, there are lots of shades of red.

Other than trying to take a cell phone away from a teenager, perhaps the most difficult communicative task a hunter can undertake is explaining to his wife why he needs to spend $1600 on a fifth rifle. If you can come up with any ideas, please contact me.

# 17.

# PISCATORIAL NOMENCLATURE, YANKEES, ERNEST HEMINGWAY, THE MAFIA AND OTHER FUN STUFF

**W**arning: If you are a practicing disciple of political correctness, do not read past this first paragraph. Go buy a Cosmopolitan or People magazine. The adherents of this movement are in a headlong rush to create utopian equality by eradicating all speech which may insult someone or hurt their fragile feelings. This practice is against human nature and common sense, as any good third grader will tell you. If you are into P.C. and ignore this admonition, you may experience terminal apoplexy.

It is amazing that we fishermen cannot come up with specific, dedicated names for the focus of our sport. For instance, some people call crappie, "white perch." There are no perch in the Deep South. What's up with that? Worse, in Louisiana, they call them "calico perch." Now, I've seen the TV series, Swamp People, and those folks can call any fish anything they want, with no argument from me. Further, we can't even get our pronunciations right. Southerners say "croppie" instead of "crappy" out of deference to our womenfolk because the latter is not used in polite company. Yankees, without such social graces, just come right out and say it, like heathens. They can use it interchangeably for the name of the fish and for a bad day of fishing.

My lifelong friend, Ducky Jones, does not like Yankees. Not because of who they are, but what they might do. He assumes that if they all knew what the weather was like down here and how good the fishing is year-round, they would all move south, overpopulating us and ruining our prolific sport. He has a valid point. No one ever says, "Hey Maude. I'm retiring soon. What say we move to Minnesota and only come out of the house 3 weeks a year?" It's cold up there. Cold can kill you. If you have the sense God gave a goat, heat will not kill you. I saw snow once. I didn't like it much.

Ducky and I were at a lakeside restaurant recently and a vacationing Yankee sitting at a nearby table asked us about some fish mounted on the wall. "Is dem crappies?" he inquired. "Croppie," Ducky corrected. The visitor bragged, "At home, we cot ours outta a ice hole." Ducky suggested that's where he would like to kick him.

Ducky has this thing all worked out. He is formulating an idea that legislation should be introduced into each Southern state that would forbid Yankees from remaining here after a visit. Florida would be exempt since it is full of them already and is Southern by geography only. He has even come up with a test for those whose origins are debatable to determine if they are truly Southern.

It consists of 3 simple questions. The people taking the test (Ducky wanted to call them "testees," but I explained that might be improper.) must answer each correctly or be sent packing. #1. Who was the winner of the last NASCAR race? #2. What is Elvis Presley's middle name? #3. What is kudzu? I told Ducky if they answer "grit vines" to #3, they have been talking to me. I tell that to every Yankee I meet. Just for kicks and grins.

I advised Ducky there was a quick field test that would replace his #3 question evaluation. Just ask the Yankee to repeat the sentence "Park the car in the yard," Since a lot of them do not pronounce the "r" in words (except for place names like Americar and Cuber) they can be readily identified. If they repeat "Pahk da cah in da yahd," they are Yankees. If they ask what a yard is, they are big city Yankees. If they ask what a car is, they are Cajuns. Run away.

Understand, I have nothing against Yankees. I married one. She is the certified, card-carrying kind. She is of Italian descent, born and raised in Cleveland and from a huge family. When they have a reunion, a large mob....I mean, bunch of people show up. At the last one, I met two of her uncles—Fat Tony and Crazy Joe Canoli. I am very careful not to say anything to or about my wife which could be construed as derogatory. I refer to our pairing as an intersectional marriage. She refers to it as interspecies. (She still checks occasionally to make sure I have opposable thumbs.)

When we first met, in Florida, where she was vacationing (of course), I asked her about her experience with fishing. She said her only involvement with fish is that she ate them every Friday in Catholic school and *The Old Man and the Sea* was on a required reading list there. She said she did not like either the meals or the book very much. I should have left at that point, but she was wearing a bikini, so instead, I interposed that I did not realize she was Catholic. She said her middle name was Marie and she had five sisters with the same middle name. Point taken.

I graduated high school in Alabama with a senior class of about 500 students. Only 2 were Catholic, but we, too, by federal mandate, had fish every Friday. However, our lunchroom personnel were creative. They simply molded hamburger into the shape of a tiny tuna. No one ever caught on. It was hilarious. I never told my wife about that because she talks on the phone to her family all the time and her uncles know where we live.

But I digress. Why does everyone say Northern Pike? Is there a Southern Pike? Just sayin'. We do have one of its second cousins here called a Chain Pickerel, or, you guessed it, a Pike. When will this madness end? Another rare denizen of the deep down here, which exemplifies our inability to settle on a name, is a black and green iridescent prehistoric thing that looks like a deformed eel on steroids called a Bowfin, also known as a Grinnell. Both the Pickerel and the Bowfin are so rarely caught, one might be tempted to lip-land them like a bass. You will only do it once. And you will not call it by any of the above names. It will henceforth be known to you as a mean*#sob#na*@!Ixing fish.

Stumpknockers are a sunfish, fairly common in shallow, warm Southern waters. They look like a cross between a bluegill and a small largemouth and are often called Rock Bass. In the Carolinas (Or Caroliners, as the Yankees would say), Saltwater Stripes are also known as Rock Bass. Stumpknockers weigh an average of 12 ounces. Saltwater Stripes weigh an average of 12 pounds. Do you begin to see the problem?

What if a fisherman from Raleigh and a fisherman from Montgomery were talking and the Carolinian was bragging about the 20-pound Rock Bass he caught? Surely, a fight would ensue. Especially if alcohol were involved, as is common with fishermen conversing about their exploits.

The many subspecies of bream is another point of consternation. We pronounce that word "Brim," but in the British Isles, where the term originated, "Bream" rhymes with "cream." And they classify it as a "course fish," as opposed to a "game fish," which is reserved exclusively for trout. Snobby chaps, the Brits. One would think that folks whose golf courses look like unkempt cow pastures would not be so condescending. I fully understand the need to differentiate between subspecies of bream, but is it a Shellcracker or a Redear?

And we can't just willy-nilly call a bass a bass. Is it a Spotted Bass or a Spot (which is the same name for a minnow used to fish for it) or a Kentucky? Is it a Smallmouth or a Bronzeback? Is it a White Bass or a Freshwater Stripe? (And that one isn't even a bass!) Did you know there is a bass subspecies called a Guadalupe? It is found in the Rio Grande River. I think it is only legal for border patrol agents to catch them on the Texas side. But I could be wrong.

I can personally attest that name consolidation can be a good thing. I once caught a 3-pound Redeye Bass (which had at least 3 other names), took it home, cleaned it and ate it. I was reading the IGFA list a few days later and discovered the world record Redeye weighed only 2 pounds. That's the only time in my life I got indigestion a week after the meal that caused it. Oh, c'mon, you know you would love to have your name in the record books. Anyway, a few years later, they changed the classification of "Redeye" to "Coosa." Technically, I rationalized, I caught a world record Redeye, but now don't feel so bad because they don't exist anymore.

So, things are getting better, I suppose. They have been worse. When I was a lad, some people called bass, "green trout." Even then, I knew there was as much difference between a bass and a trout as between me and a monkey. (My wife might challenge that analogy.) Those same folks used the term "trout line" instead of "trot line." Fortunately, most of those people married their first cousins and their blood lines are slowly being eradicated.

If you have any idea on how we can correct this nomenclature mess, please let me know. But hurry. I may not be here much longer. In this one article alone, I have managed to offend everyone north of the Mason-Dixon line, the entire population of at least two states and a couple of sovereign nations, a popular political movement and a global religion, not to mention the Mafia and some of my neighbors. I may end up surrounded by crime scene tape and a cop with a baton will be saying, "Move along. Nothing to see here." But a passerby will ask, "What was his name?" And the cop will answer, "I'm not sure."

# 18.

# SQUIRRELS AND
# OTHER DANGEROUS ANIMALS

As the weather turns cooler and Ducky so disturbingly observes, "Have you noticed that it gets later earlier this time of year?," my thoughts turn to small game hunting. I have many fond memories of days afield pursuing the lesser but more prolific targets of our sport. But I also have recollections that are not so pleasant.

Now, you wouldn't think a two-pound furry little mammal could be considered injurious and excluding the rare time when some dufus (like me) picks up a live bushytail that was only knocked senseless from a 30-foot fall and it starts gnawing on your knuckles with its little beaver teeth, you would be correct. Or excluding the time you actually put the very much still alive creature in your game vest, and it tries to claw its way through your back, squirrels are not a dangerous lot. But the mere act of looking for the things can be downright deadly since you are forever peering upwards.

Since you are probably not so easily befuddled as am I, this may have never happened to you. If it has, don't tell anyone. On more than one occasion, I have been walking through the woods searching for the elusive greys when my gaze finally dropped from the treetops, and I looked around to discover I had not a clue where I was. I might as well have been deposited into the middle of a Central American rainforest. Thick tree canopy, thicker clouds and not a landmark in sight. You know, one of those situations that would convert a devout atheist.

It is difficult for even a rational person to control panic in such a scenario. Now I have been accused of being many things, but rational has rarely been one of them. It's very late in the day, and even the muted sounds of a distant highway have vanished, and I am standing thigh deep in dark tannic swamp water I do not even remember entering. To reassure myself, I kept repeating, "It's alright. It's alright. It's alright." Over a lifetime of observation, I have noticed that if someone says "It's alright more than ten times in a row, it's usually not alright.

I picked a direction, immediately to my rear, and started out. But, impossibly, the water got deeper. Hard left. Deeper still. About face. It gradually got more shallow until I was standing on (semi) dry land. I glanced around to make sure I had not entered the property upon which Black Water Hattie's shack sat. I saw no such structure, but my relief was brief. Speaking of briefs, I almost ruined mine when I looked down and saw my pants were covered in leeches.

Now everyone, whether they admit it or not, has an irrational fear of something. My wife is deathly afraid of roaches. I grew up in the South and can name five species of the things. A few made a permanent residence in the tool shed out back of my childhood home and I named several of them. Ralph and Robbie are the only two I remember. Ducky is petrified of spiders. Once, when a tiny one ran by his foot in a crowded restaurant, he screeched like a bad set of truck brakes and knocked a waiter and an old lady down on his way out the door.

But leeches! Slimy, writhing little bloodsuckers. I started to sit down on that patch of land I had stumbled upon and pick them off before they got to bare skin. Then I noticed the little island was slightly moving. Thinking it was panic-induced insanity, I blinked a few times in the deepening twilight and realized it was literally alive with snakes. It was then I jumped up and sloshed and splashed back into the water with my friends the leeches.

Somehow and somewhat surprisingly I finally slogged my way out. At one point, I stopped and searched for the sun that had already gone down and noticed the scores of squirrels in the trees. I was so far back in the wilderness, they were almost tame, never having seen a human being before. (They never saw this one again.) I swear some of them were laughing.

Now, there is a way to hunt squirrels and not fall to the scourge of blind disorientation. Simply use a dog. I have had a couple or three, but they were always subject to gross distraction. In the middle of the hunt, they became chipmunk dogs, sparrow dogs and turtle dogs. One even had a fixation on oddly shaped limbs. Ducky thinks he has hit upon the ideal canine for squirrel hunting—the dachshund. And they don't even have to do anything but frolic through the woods. This is his theory. Squirrels make difficult targets. They are frisky critters, forever scurrying through the branches at top speed when a wiener dog comes trotting underneath, Mr. Squirrel stops dead in its tracks, looks down and says, "What the hell is that?" Stationary target. Boom.

If you are hunting without a dog, another deadly small game is the quail. Any cardiologist worth his medical degree will war dogless quail hunters of the dangers involved in this activity. On a still, quiet, cool morning, nothing is quite as potentially terminal as having the earth erupt underneath your feet in a thunderous explosion of beating wings. I myself started considering bird dogs when I noticed I couldn't raise my gun stock to my shoulder until my heart started beating again. When the interval between covey break and trigger pull exceeded 30 seconds, I started using pointers.

Another hazardous activity is rabbit hunting. You wouldn't think a floppy-eared, cotton-tailed little thing like Mr. Bunny, the theme of Easter tunes, could be so precarious. And physically, he's not, if you are hunting by yourself. However, if you are pursuing him with a partner, which most of us do, rabbits, too, can be deadly. See, they have somehow developed, over the millennia, the uncanny ability to usually run directly between two hunters, both of whom at some point will be aiming in each other's direction. I think it is an evolved innate survival skill nature has given them.

Speaking of shooting each other, we cannot leave the dove out of this discussion. Now, most every dove hunter has been peppered with bird shot at one time or another and it does not result in mortal wounds. And if you have been doing it a long time, you might even have some #8's under your skin somewhere on your body. Ducky has been shot so many times that he uses it as a pickup line for women (between marriages). "Hey, you wanna see some lead shot I got in my shoulder?"

I didn't say it was a good pickup line. And I've never seen it work for him, but he keeps trying. Ducky's standards aren't too high anyway. Remember, he has one ex-wife who was severely injured in a freak pole-dancing accident. Anyway, dove hunting does not present a serious physical danger for its adherents. The treachery of this sport is the emotional damage, especially among novices, often resulting in the destruction of equipment.

You've seen it. Poor fellow down the field goes through two boxes of shells and nary a feather falls. It takes a toll on people. I have personally witnessed two perfectly innocent shotguns shattered on fence posts. And once, I saw a fellow empty his Bernelli into his shooting stool, then grab it by the barrel for leverage and throw it into a pond. A Bernelli! Perhaps the saddest exhibit though was the time a medical doctor had a full-fledged mental breakdown. He had to be escorted from the field, blubbering and crying, "They're so fast! How can they be so fast?" I heard he had to be institutionalized for a while.

Of course, these aren't the only small game that should be considered dangerous. We could include the woodcock, but they are more rare than a fashion designer in China. And Ducky is the only person I know who actually hunts possum. (For his traditional Christmas dinner.) And I have disparaged coon hunters so much over the years, I fear they actually have a cash bounty out on me, so I won't speak ill of the coon.

However, I'll leave you with this. Remember the words of my wise old grandpa. "If ya go ta kill a skunk, boy, ya better ought not miss."

# 19.

# ALTERNATIVES

Several years ago, Ducky and I were pulling our boat out at Furter's Landing, when the owner, Frank, (yes, that's his real name and he has a couple of unflattering nicknames to go with it) came trotting down to the ramp in a semi-panic. He quickly related that both the soft-drink vendor and the beer vendor had showed up at the same time and he didn't have enough money to cover his bill. He asked if one of us wanted to buy his trash truck.

He called it that because he used it to haul trash from the marina. But it was a fitting name because it was a piece of ... well, trash. A 1948 Chevy pickup, rusted almost beyond recognition as a mode of transportation and held together with duct tape and chicken wire. No passenger side floorboard. I don't mean it had a hole in it. I mean it didn't exist. Whoever was brave enough to sit there had to brace his feet on the dashboard, watch the pavement whiz by underneath and pray he didn't slide out.

But it would crank, it would run, and it would move. I wrote him a check for $100 and Ducky drove his truck and my boat home, and I drove the Jammerator. That is the name we gave to it because you had to slam the brake pedal all the way to the floorboard to get it to stop. The transmission wasn't strong enough to pull a boat, so Ducky and I decided to use it for pond fishing. It was ideal for dirt roads, rutted roads, mud roads, no roads and cow pastures. We no longer had to take our good trucks and risk a broken axle, a clogged air filter, or scratches to the paint. It was the perfect alternative.

Except, of course, it had no modern shocks and the springs that substituted for them had long since become immobilized with oxidized accretions. The ride was jolting, to say the least. For the driver, it was uncomfortable. For the passenger, it was terrifying. Any moment, you could be cast out through the bottom of the vehicle. We argued a lot about who would drive.

The Jammerator was a hoot to take around town on short errands. It confounded the traffic cops because it didn't look street legal, but it was. Sometimes, they would pull you over and look for 20 minutes trying to find something they could ticket you for. None did. Having a vehicle that is four different colors is not against the law. And it would horrify dogs that normally chased cars. They would actually run away and cower on their porches. Sitting at a traffic light, it shook like a paint can mixer and the fan belt would, without warning, shriek like a cat caught under a riding mower. That once scared a guy in the crosswalk so bad, I swear he levitated. I leaned out the window and apologized. He said it was O.K. It reminded him his wife had wanted him to pick up some toilet paper.

I kept the Jammerator for several months and the only money I spent on it was for gas and the mandatory quart of oil every 40 miles. And I bought a used recap when the left rear exploded downtown. They closed the courthouse that day under a terrorist attack protocol. Oh, yeah, I had to buy a few stove bolts to reattach the driver's side door when it fell off in the middle of an intersection. That was exciting. And I gave it some class with a 25-cent glass steering knob I picked up at a yard sale.

Frank called me one day and wanted to buy it back because the health department was on him about the garbage piling up behind the marina. I sold it back to him for $150. (For those of you who are not mathematically inclined, that's a $50 profit.) Frank was a little reluctant at first, but then he spotted the steering wheel knob and said, "Nice touch." I thought so too.

Mr. Furter sold his place a couple of years after that transaction and retired. We went to his retirement party, and I mentioned to him that now he would be able to fish every day. Frank loved to fish. Surprisingly, he said he was through with fishing. I was so shocked; I don't even remember my response. He said after living a barely minimal hand-to-mouth existence with the sport for over two decades, he had developed a deep psychological aversion to fishing. I was incredulous and might have been crying. "What on earth are you going to do?," I whined. He thought for a moment and said, "Maybe darts." That was disturbing.

After the party, Ducky and I went back to his place and retired to his veranda, still in shock at Frank's decision. We opened a brand-new bottle of Kentucky's finest and discussed the ramifications of such a resolution. We looked at each other and simultaneously said, "Darts?" I asked Ducky what sport he would pursue if he couldn't fish anymore. He got that expression on his face as if he were severely constipated and could not seem to grasp the question.

"Why on earth would I quit fishing?" he finally asked. "I don't know. What if you suddenly became allergic to water?" and almost immediately realized the absurdity of the question. If that happened, you would have much bigger problems than choosing an alternative to fishing. "O.K., suppose PETA took over the government and outlawed fishing?" I queried. Without hesitation, Ducky said, "I would be on 'America's Most Wanted' every week." I retorted, "O.K., O.K., forget the reason. If you absolutely had to quit fishing, what would you replace it with?" We sat silently for a while and mulled and drank. Then we drank and mulled. Surprisingly, we came up with some possibilities.

Ducky said he had thought about taking up golf once but had tried it and hated it. I told him if he hated it the first time, he would really, really despise it the second time. If you are not familiar with it, golf is an insidious little game invented by Scottish gnomes and intended to completely destroy the human ego. "Par" is a golf term meaning "average." You are beat before you begin. Only 2% of the population can score par on any given hole.

The week before you play your Saturday round of golf, you could have closed the Covington account, earning a hefty bonus, successfully changed the spark plugs on your car without skinning your knuckles and have been praised by your mother-in-law for being such a fine husband. Great, huh? After you finish your golf round, you will feel lower than the barometric pressure in a Category 5 hurricane. And the really bad thing is you will accidently sink a miraculous 40-foot putt on the 18th green and that's the only stroke you will remember when you are invited to go next weekend. It is addictive. And it tricks you into thinking you can be good at it. You can't.

After about his third libation, Ducky said if he couldn't fish, he thought he might take up drinking as a full-time sport. I told him it took a long time to become an expert, and he didn't consume nearly enough alcohol to even be considered for membership in that club. If you have to ask, "Is it too early to start?" you are considered a rank amateur and will only be scoffed at by the pros.

I suggested tennis. Ducky groaned. I said, "Think about it. We already have mastered the overhead, sidearm and backhand casts. Those are the primary swings of the tennis racket." Ducky sneered and replied, "But you have to wear those sissy shorts and pastel-colored shirts." I remembered, "Oh, yeah." So much for tennis.

Ducky sat up and said, "I've got it! We could become race car fans!" I said, "What do you mean "we" Gringo?" I am possibly the only Southern male on the underside of Nashville that is not a devotee of NASCAR. I simply find watching vehicles going around in a perpetual circle to be tantamount to watching clothes dry. Now, I understand the concept of going fast, but so what? In a recent sports column, I saw it referred to as "speed racing." What other kind is there? 'Racing' indicates 'going fast' and 'speed' means 'going fast' so the words are synonymous and redundant. It's like saying "fishing for fish." If they really wanted to make the Indy 500 interesting, they would have the cars pull bass boats. It wouldn't be as fast, but the wrecks would be spectacular.

Ducky and I sat long into the night in our effort to come up with an alternative to fishing. We considered bowling, but Ducky nixed it because he says he never picks up anything that weighs more than 5 pounds. Claims that is the secret to a long life. I asked him, "What about a 6-pound bass?" He said, "Except that." We considered soccer, but I discounted that immediately because it is unnatural to play any game involving a ball that you cannot touch with your hands. I think there's something in the Bible about it.

After Ducky went to sleep in his lawn chair, I stared at the stars for a while in deep contemplation and decided that if for some unearthly and unforeseen reason, I had to give up fishing, I would take up buying and selling trash trucks for a hobby.

# 20.

# TURKEY TALK

**D**ucky Jones and I were sitting in my den the other evening, sipping a cold beverage, and discussing the finer points of shotgun chokes, turkey loads and roost locations, when the news came on the television and the subject of "gun control" reared its ugly head yet again. I told him those were the scariest words in the English language. He disagreed, arguing that the scariest words were, "Run! It's Bigfo...." I had to give him that one.

Some government official twit on TV was explaining to a sympathetic news anchor and to we great unwashed moron viewers that the second amendment was written to provide a well-regulated militia, or as he said, "a group of neighborhood policemen." Ducky and I sat with our mouths open. He continued his interview with his notion of how to stop all of the murders happening around our nation. "If we outlaw the manufacture of magazines, as soon as the existing ones are used up, there will be no more ammo." Ducky and I looked at each other in stunned silence. The interviewer mentioned that most murders were committed with handguns, not rifles. The elected Cretin ignored that. Then he said that automatic rifles had to be banned. The newsman told him sheepishly and rather quietly that automatic weapons had been banned decades ago. The idiot politician got a strange look on his face, and they cut to a commercial.

Ducky said to the TV, "Please come try to take my guns. Please!" I said, "They can't hear you, Duck," to which he replied, They will.

Oh, they will." I shut off the distracting television before they came back on, and Ducky had to buy me a new one. "Let's let sleeping politicians lie," I said. He said, "Oh, they're going to lie whether they're sleeping or not." I said, "Speaking of turkeys, would you like to go hunting for them tomorrow?" He brightened. "Do they sell fleas at a flea market?" I said, "Well actually they don't" He said quickly, "Well, I want to go anyway." You've never had fun until you've heard my deaf wife and her equally deaf husband carry on a conversation from different rooms.

I yelled to her from the den, "Honey, Ducky and I are going hunting in the morning!" She yelled back, "I don't know where you're going running in the corn! That's a cotton field out back!" I replied, "If there's rotten meal in the sack, it's gone! I already took the trash out!" "Stay out of my purse and put that money right back!" "O.K., we should be no later than noon!" Ducky was sitting with this puzzled look on his face. "What the hell was that all about?' I said, "We're going hunting in the morning!" He mumbled something about just having heard more senseless gobbling than he would hear all season.

Early the next morning, he had his chance to prove it. The sky was just beginning to lighten, we were sitting side by side, completely still and camouflaged, with our backs against a huge oak overlooking a hardwood bottom. He was working a diaphragm call expertly. I imagined him saying, "Come here Tom. Let me have a look at that big beard." Or maybe not. I'm an old man. I have a vivid imagination.

We sat motionless for two hours with no sight of or sound from Mr. Gobbler. Then, even I heard the rustling in the dry leaves from our right front coming along the ridge, getting slowly louder. We were completely silent and still. Then we saw them. Two young teenagers, creeping along slowly, 22 single shots in hand, searching the treetops for squirrels. They were about 20 yards in front of us and had no idea we were there. You had to smile at their inexperience, but when I glanced at Ducky, I noticed his smile was more of an evil, mischievous grin. He glanced at me, and I quickly nodded an almost imperceptible but unmistakable "No!"

I know Ducky. He wanted to yell "Hey!" as loud as he could, watch them soil themselves and sprint downhill as fast as their spindly legs would carry them. But I knew there was always the chance that they would turn and open up on us in blind, panic induced terror. Fortunately, Ducky kept his stupid mouth shut and we avoided the newspaper headlines "Two Local Wives Finally Report Their Husbands Missing After Three Weeks." The kids wandered out of sight, clueless that we were ever there.

We sat and Ducky called. And Ducky called and we sat. Finally, he whispered, "My butt's sore." I whispered back, "Yeah, I thought I heard it grow" and wrinkled my nose. Just as that exchange had taken place, we heard a tentative rustling behind us, and we became sitting statues. Not even a blink. Frozen in anticipation at least equal to that of a groom on his wedding night. (I told you. I'm an old man.)

And what should come ambling by, on my side of the tree, about 5 feet away, but a skunk. Now we were frozen in fear. I know hunters who have gone an entire lifetime without ever seeing a skunk in the wild. I have seen exactly four. And every one of them appeared in the exact situation I was in then. And almost at the same distance. Now, I suppose the odds of that are about the same as being trampled to death by a flock of feral chickens, but it's true! If you've never been sprayed from close range, let me explain that there is not enough lemon extract, tomato juice or expensive French perfume in the Western Hemisphere to allow you to return to civilization for a week. And all that expensive camo and those boots? Dumpster. Seat covers in your vehicle? Replaced. (If you can find an upholsterer with an olfactory disability.) Going home? Tent in the backyard.

Fortunately, Pepe LePew only stopped briefly to sniff the air, ostensibly catching the scent of Ducky's aforementioned flatulence and, thinking a possible mate had passed by, scurried off in the direction the teenagers had taken, searching for his new love. We breathed a sigh of relief. Not long afterwards, we heard the crack of two rifle shots, an ungodly scream, lots of words a kid's mother would not have tolerated and then watched as they ran flat-out and wide open below us, hysterical to the point of insanity.

We laughed, long and loud. I know, I know. That was wrong. But it was hilarious. Only one of them had his rifle. I'm sure the other was thrown at the little animal in sheer desperation or perhaps he decided he could run faster without it. After we wiped our eyes, Ducky finally said, "I guess those are the only two turkeys in the woods today." We left.

I think I've told you before that Ducky is the eternal optimist. On the ride home, I told him, "Sorry we didn't get a bird today, Duck." He replied, "Oh, that's not important. I had a great time. We didn't get a Tom, but then again, we didn't get skunk sprayed. And we had a good belly laugh watching those kids run. And unlike one of them, we left the woods with our guns. Speaking of which, not one time this morning did I think about those progressive brain-dead politicians who want to take them away. And we didn't waste any ammo, did we? I had a great time!" He paused a minute and then said, "There's a restaurant up ahead that serves a mean turkey and dressing lunch. My treat. What 'cha say?"

The only appropriate thing I could say, was "Gobble, gobble."

# 21.

# TIS THE SEASON

Christmas can be a stressful and even contentious time of year, especially for sportsmen. So, I am herein humbly offering some hints that may benefit you in this holiday season. Gift giving is an aspect of Christmas that can present some real problems. For instance, guys, if your wife does not hunt, do not get her a duck call, an AR15, or size 12 waterproof boots. She'll see right through it. Trust me, I know. And don't buy her camouflage panties and matching bra. You might think they are sexy, but again, trust me.

And ladies, don't get your husband a necktie with a picture of a salmon on it. Outdoorsmen do not like neckties and there are no salmon in the Deep South. And if you don't participate in his chosen sport, tell the clerk at the sporting goods store what your husband's preference is, and he will help you out. That way, you won't end up buying a case of dove shot for a deer hunter.

And if you are like a lot of wives and don't ask him what he wants so the gift will be a total surprise, do some snooping around, so you won't duplicate something he already has. You might not know about that $950 Bernelli he bought himself last year. But don't fuss at him. It's Christmas.

And guys, if she does ask what you want for Christmas, it is sometimes difficult to balance between vague description and direct specification. Always err on the side of exact identification. Otherwise, bad things can happen. I once told my wife I needed a new rod and reel. I ended up with a pink Zebco 202 with a picture of Daffy Duck on it.

Speaking of ducks, the wife of my friend Ducky Jones complained to me that he is a very difficult person for which to buy. Last Christmas, she wanted to get him an all-weather hunting cap, but he wouldn't give her his hat size. So, I got him aside and asked him why. He said that the government already knew too much about him, and he didn't want to disseminate any more vital statistics to them.

I said, "Ducky. Why would the government find out your hat size if you told your wife?" He said, "She's got a big mouth." "O.K.," I patiently responded, "why does it matter if the government knows your hat size?" "Because" Ducky impatiently answered, "they can calculate the size of my brain." I told him I could already do that. It's tiny.

Christmas gift giving was so much simpler when we were kids. You gave Mom whatever Dad got for you to give to her. And you gave Dad a glass ashtray to which you had glued a fishing picture to the outside of the bottom. Or you got him a coffee mug that said, "World's Greatest Fisherman."

And the presents you got as a kid were almost magical. The first gun every hunter who is reading this received was a cap pistol. There was nothing like the smell of cordite on Christmas morning. We all first learned the true meaning of "keep your powder dry" with a cap pistol. And old or damp roll of caps was not only frustrating, but dangerous. Nothing could get you killed faster than two or three simultaneous misfires.

Another point of discord revolves around Christmas dinner. I think our problem comes from our memories of Christmases past and our expectations of those meals being repeated. Just accept the fact that ain't gonna happen. When I was a kid, we spent many a Christmas Day up in the country at my grandparent's farm. Dinner consisted of ham straight from the smokehouse, a turkey Grandpa had raised for the occasion and butchered the day before, home-made cornbread dressing, handmade cathead biscuits, freshly churned butter and home canned blackberry jam, topped off with fresh pecan pie. And Grandma would always say, "It ain't much. Choke it down if you can." (Whaaaaaat?!?) There was no supper. No one could eat anything for the next two days. Like I said, that is not going to happen again. Don't waste your time expecting it to.

We might try to duplicate it, but most everything comes out of a grocery store freezer and "just add water" boxes. Way back when, after Christmas dinner, Grandpa would retire to his rocking chair in front of the fireplace and have his hot toddy. To make modern Christmas dinners more palatable, I have taken to having a toddy or two before dinner. I highly recommend it.

My aforementioned friend Ducky has, over the years, developed his own unique Christmas dinner and managed to make it a tradition with his family. It consists mainly of possum and sweet potatoes. I haven't eaten Christmas dinner at Ducky's house in over 20 years. If you've never tasted it, possum is greasier than goat and eating goat is like ladling lard straight out of the can.

I have had to get very creative to turn down Ducky's invitations to Christmas dinner. Since he dislikes my mother-in-law even more than I do, I once told him, "I would love to come, Ducky and since my wife's mother is visiting, I'll br...."""Oh, wait a minute, I forgot. We're going out of town this Christmas. We'll do it next year." Some of my excuses have not been so immediately successful. I once told him I couldn't come to his dinner because possum gives me diarrhea. He told me not to worry because the sweet potatoes would constipate me. It's hard to argue with Ducky.

Another activity that can cause complications is the Christmas tree. Now, any fool can cut one down. But if you're like me, the problem arises in building a base that can keep said tree upright. Personally, any of my trees that lean at less than a 45-degree angle are considered to be a huge success. If you have this problem, there are two viable alternatives: Get a degree in engineering or buy a metal stand. The latter is cheaper. I have tried neither. I am too stupid to get an engineering degree and too stingy to buy something I will only use once a year. My wife calls me Ebenezer.

But tis the season. Enjoy it. Despite the attendant problems, I can say that Christmas has made me more creative. Everyone in my large extended family knows I love to fish and consequently I get a lot of duplicate gifts. Last year, I got three tackle boxes. After much consideration about how to utilize them all, I took two and used them to store the extra fish neckties and "World's Greatest Fisherman" coffee mugs.

# 22.

# THE NOT SO VERY
# MIDAS TOUCH OF DUCKY JONES

**D**ucky told me the other day he was working on his second million dollars. I knew what was coming but played along and told him I was not aware that he had made his first million. "I haven't," he admitted. "It was too hard." I didn't want to ruin that old joke for him. Ducky can be so sensitive, and sometimes it's not pretty. Ducky and I are both retired but still work to supplement our incomes. I, of course, write, and Ducky builds birdhouses. Needless to say, neither of us make much money.

I used to have a complete command of the English language but now have to have a dictionary and a thesaurus just to write a grocery list, so I don't see any bestselling novels or a lot of cash in my future. Ducky, on the other hand, is obsessed with getting rich but, since birdhouses don't bring in much, he has taken to other creative measures to achieve prosperity, including inventions.

His most recent idea is this. He figures that since doe season is becoming more and more popular and since the deer herds keep growing, it won't be long before there will be a spotted fawn season. In anticipation of that, he has been buying up a stock of decorative plastic butterflies to which he attaches little alligator clips on the bottoms. I suppose he has been reminiscing about old Disney movies and assumes that spotted fawns walk through the forest sniffing butterflies on bushes. In Ducky's strange head, the hunter will simply attach his plastic decoys to the vegetation surrounding his blind or tree stand and when said fawn stops to take a whiff, Boom! He is going to call them Bambi Busters.

I told Ducky, "Hunters aren't going to buy that."

"Sure, they will. They buy camo boxer shorts, for God's sake. They'll buy anything!"

"No, Ducky. I mean they're not going to hunt spotted fawns."

"Why not? It'll be legal!"

"First of all, you are as crazy as a football bat if you think there is ever going to be a season for spotted fawns. And second of all, Southern hunters, despite their gruff exterior and questionable judgement in choosing mates and cologne, are, above all, Southern gentlemen. And they are not going to harvest the young of any species, legal or not."

Ducky thought for a minute. "Oh." Then he thought for another minute. "Well, what am I going to do with 8 gross of boxed butterflies in my garage?"

Then I thought for a minute. "Burn your garage down?" He just stared at me with that deadpan look he gets, like he's severely constipated but hasn't given up yet. I asked him how much he had paid for them. "A buck fifty each," he replied, disgustedly.

Why don't you put one on each of your birdhouses? You can just bump the price up to cover the cost of your butterfly investment." He studied for a moment, counted on his fingers and looked down at his toes. "So, your saying after I build one thousand, one hundred a fifty birdhouses, I'll break even on the butterflies?" I nodded. He frowned and continued. "So, at five birdhouses a week, it'll only take a little over 4 years to get my butterfly money back?" I nodded again. He relaxed, grinned, and said, "Brilliant, brother!" Like I've told you before, Ducky is the eternal optimist.

A while later, he came up with the idea of starting a podcast and giving hunting and fishing tips to the millions of outdoorsmen he imagines are sitting around waiting on his expertise. "I've heard podcasts can be very lucrative. I could make a fortune!"

"Ducky, do you remember last week when you called me because you forgot how to turn your computer on?" "Yeah. But that was the morning after Jenkin's birthday party. I also forgot I was married there for a while." "O.K., do you remember week before last when you hit the wrong key on your computer and deleted your entire email history?"

He hung his head. "Yeah."

"And do you remember..."

He interrupted, "O.K., O.K.." His head got lower.

"You don't have a clue how to set up a podcast, do you?"

A barely audible "No" came out.

"Neither do I. Let's go fishing." And we did.

He's had other great ideas. Like the time he came up with the notion of a cookbook for the outdoorsman. He said, "It will be for those with a discriminating taste and a refined palate." I told him, "Ducky, your target customer is not going to be a New York restaurant critic. It is going to be hunters and fishermen. They have three degrees of taste: good, not good, and spit it the hell out. Secondly, your signature dish is Notnuff Stew. It would take over a hundred pages just to list the possible ingredients, some of which you do not even know the name of. And do you remember the time you put hulled acorns in that concoction and almost killed us all? You'll be sued before the ink is dry on your cookbook. And besides that, specially stew, what other chapters are you going to include? 'How to put bottled barbeque sauce on boiled squirrel"? The Art of seasoning bass with salt and pepper'? Oh, I know, ' Baking without a pan'. That will be a ...." He interrupted. "Stop, stop. I see your point." He sighed loudly. I hate it when he does that. I took him for ice cream.

In pursuit of his second million, this happens at least once a week. There's a rapid knock on the door and there is Ducky's smiling face. "Hey, what about this? You know how you put a rod in a holder when you're bottom fishing from the bank and you tie a little bell to the rod tip to detect a strike? Well, what if that bell was a little electronic buzzer?"

"Already been done, Duck." "Really?" "Yeah."

"Hey, what about this? A lighted tackle box for night fishing?"

"Already been done, Duck." "Really?" "Yeah. Sorry."

"Hey, what about this? You know all those neckties the grandkids give us with a picture of a leaping bass on them? What if we painted those bass with that translucent silver sparkly glue so that the scales of the fish actually shine?"

"Ducky, I think you may have something there."

All that glitters is not gold.

# 23.

# THE CASE OF THE MISSING TALE

It was a dark and stormy night. The seven or eight of us had arrived at our deer club cabin on Friday evening to get a good night's sleep before our big weekend whitetail hunt. The cabin isn't much to look at. The roof and outside walls are interchangeable, but we have 4 large rooms, two of which are dedicated to sleeping cots and single wide beds plus a closet with a toilet in it and a really big fireplace in the main room. And despite the current prevailing political atmosphere, there is a sign on the front door that reads "No Women Allowed." They would never find us out there anyway.

Someone mentioned that on the way there, they had listened to the weather forecast on the radio, and it looked as if the cold wind and rain and thunder and lightning would last all night. That was O.K.. We had assigned our newest member, Mark, as per protocol, to provide supper and he had responded with a half-dozen pizzas. Meals for the remainder of the weekend would either be fresh venison or the canned beans and Vienna sausage we had purchased in quantity at the beginning of the season and kept stored there. Due to either bad luck or bad aim, we were running real, real low on the canned goods.

Ducky and Jake Jenkins and I are legacy members of the club, and we can pick and choose who we want for membership without a club vote. We had met the bearer of the pizzas, Mark, a couple of weeks earlier at a local watering hole and Jake and I had taken an instant liking to him and wanted to invite him for membership.

Ducky, being Ducky, was reluctant and suspicious. So, he tested the new guy as only Ducky could or would. Now, Mark is a large, muscular and imposing younger man, but Ducky told him his name sounded like a dog with a speech defect. Instead of getting up and beating the crap out of Ducky, Mark laughed and said he was just happy not to be named after a waterfowl. He was in the club.

Did I mention it was a dark and stormy night? I realize that was Snoopy's opening line for every novel he pounded out on his typewriter while he sat on his doghouse, but it is very important for this storyline since it sets the mood for a spooky, mysterious narrative. Since we have no radio or TV in the cabin due to club rules, obviously created after several rounds of Tennessee's finest, we had to rely on conversation for entertainment. In our initial quest for really "roughing it" and removing ourselves from civilization, we don't even allow cell phones there.

Not that Ducky or Jenkins or I even have one. When you are old and retired and boring and tired of answering robo calls from Medicare providers, there is no longer a need for one. I mentioned this little fact to a pharmacist one day, when he requested my cell number for some reason only pharmacists and bankers and insurance agents know and when I told him of my lack thereof, I might as well have said I came from a planet in the Borzak star system and had a third eye in the back of my head. He was speechless. Which he would have been had he called my non-existent cell phone anyway.

Back to the dark and stormy night. We had the fireplace roaring in no time with a treasured particulate processed starter log. No more lightered, shavings, twigs and precise stacking. Just put a store-bought fake on the grate, cover it with split wood and fire it up. We gathered around the fireplace on various pieces of used furniture and munched pepperoni pizza. Jake said, "This will be a good evening for some 'dark and stormy night' stories, boys." Somebody added "And cold." Mark snorted and said, "You don't know what cold is."

Everyone looked at Mark with raised eyebrows as if to take exception to that particular statement. He explained, "Now it doesn't get really cold in LA very often, but when it does..." Someone interrupted, "I didn't know you were from California!" (That last word sounded as if he had something nasty in his mouth.) I countered, "He's not, you dufus! LA is Lower Alabama." "Oh," the interrupter muttered. Mack nodded his approval and continued.

"It is open plains country. Nothing stops the wind. And as I said, it doesn't get cold very often, but when it does, it would scare an Eskimo. And they put duck season right in the middle of it. One day, my older brother and I went out to a series of little farm ponds and without the wind chill, it was 15 degrees that morning. All the ponds had a rim of ice around the edges. We sat on the dam of one in the broomsage and waited. They started pouring in, mostly mallards and canvasbacks with a few woodies mixed in. We picked our shots so they would fall on dry land. We had almost gotten our limit when I got a little anxious and nailed one that fell in the water, about 10 yards from shore. We were on the lee side, so the wind would not blow him in or out. He just floated there in one spot.

My brother said, "O.K., bird dog, go get him." I told him he was crazier than a run over cat and there was no way in hell I was going in that water. He said, 'Strip down, jump in, grab the duck, get out and put your dry clothes back on. It'll take less than a minute.' I told him he had the attention span of a retarded goldfish and repeated that I was not going in that water. Then he said it. The magic words that all older siblings know and use to win every argument ever instigated. 'I'll tell Dad.'

"Now, you've got to understand that my father is not only a military veteran, but an upright, upstanding proponent of rules and regulations, especially when it comes to sportsmanship. And he ruled us boys with all the subtlety of a deranged drill sergeant. His words regarding hunting were branded in our little brains. 'Never shoot anything you are not going to eat."

Someone asked, "What did you do Mark?" He answered in a tone that implied an idiot had asked the question. "I played bird dog." Ducky said, "You know, Mark, in some states, it would not have been illegal to kill your brother." Jenkins opined, "Well, Mark, that was an interesting story. Actually, it was kind of sad more than anything. I was expecting something a little more spine-tingling. You know, bone-chilling. After all, it's a dark and stormy night."

Mark replied, "Oh, I guarantee it chilled my bones! And I promise you my spine tingled for a week. You've never been so cold you couldn't breathe, have you Jake?" Jake said, "Well, once my mother-in-law walked in on me when I was naked in my bedroom, and I swear the temperature dropped 20 degrees. And I had a hard time breathing then. But I wanted someone to regale us with a truly terrifying adventure."

Ducky spoke up. "I've been married 8 times." Most of the crowd did not know this and there was stunned silence. Then came the comments. "That is terrifying!" "To different women?!?" "And you're still here to tell about it!" "How on earth did you manage that?"

I interjected, "I'll give you a hint. I was at his house yesterday when his wife came in from shopping and asked if she had any messages. Ducky said, "Yeah, Satan called and wants you to come back immediately'. Any more questions?" Everybody's eyes got big, and they looked at Ducky in awe (some with admiration). Ducky grinned and shrugged and stated, "Someone once said that you can never be a good philosopher unless you've been married twice. I, gentlemen, am a veritable Socrates." A couple of guys applauded.

Another guy said, "I've got a mystery story, Jake. I once shot a buck that didn't have any horns." There was silence for a moment and everybody just sort of looked at him and then at each other incredulously. The men sitting on either side of him scooted away. Jake said, "You're a moron."

I jumped in. "Did I ever tell you guys about the time I got lost in the oxbow swamp?"

"Counting today, 23 times."

"When was your last brain aneurysm?"

"Do you even remember what you had for breakfast this morning?"

I replied, "As a matter of fact, I certainly do. I have the same thing for breakfast every morning so I can remember what I had for breakfast this morning." It seemed to be the prevailing opinion that I had indeed related that tale before, so I shut up.

Jenkins' young nephew spoke up from the back of the room and said, "Uncle Jake, you remember the time when I was a kid, and you took us hunting in the Florida panhandle and you came screaming back into camp one evening..."

"No, son, I don't rememb... "And you didn't have your gun and..."

"I don't recollect that at..."

"And you were trying to yell Skunk Ape, but all that came out was..."

"I told you, boy, I don't know what... "

"Stump Ache, Stunk Scape..."

Jake yelled "You must be talking about another Uncle!" He stood up quickly, stretched and said, "Time to hit the sack." As he walked off, Ducky said, "You mean 'sit the hack' don't you?" We all sat and giggled a while.

Then we, too, drifted off to bed. The wind was howling around the corner, the rain pattered on the tin roof and the thunder rumbled softly in the distance. We each dreamed of the eight pointer we would get tomorrow. It was good sleeping. After all, it was a dark and stormy night.

# 24.

# ALL ABOUT LUCK

You may hear the less intellectually inclined in our society occasionally say there is no such thing as "luck." If you hunt or fish, you know better. And if you have no manners, you will probably laugh in their face, then back away and point and scoff. And you should be excused for that. Whether you call it fortune or destiny or fate, luck most definitely exists, and it plays a big part in our lives.

If you learned anything past the third grade, you may have noticed luck comes in two categories: good and bad. Sometimes, though, those two adjectives occur almost simultaneously. I once won a brand new oversized, fully stocked tackle box at an outdoor sports show with a raffle ticket. I placed it "temporarily" on the roof of my car and drove off down I-65, never to see it again. In retrospect, there were several people who passed me, blowing their horns and pointing and waving, but I assumed it was for my "Bill Dance for President" bumper sticker.

Many times, we are not aware of our luck or lack thereof. 4:58 a.m. A twelve-point Boone and Crockett buck walks directly beneath your tree stand. 5:10 a.m. You climb into your tree stand. Never knew. An 8-pound bass is cruising the shallow bank on a still April morning, sizing up a bream bed and circling to attack when you splat a 5 inch Rapala directly on top of them. They noisily spook and scatter like cows in a lightning strike, sending said largemouth into deep water. Never knew.

There are people who know how lucky they are. They are often eccentric and believe in totems, icons or seraphic beings for reasons I have never comprehended. Ducky Jones, one of the luckiest people I have ever known, brought a stringer of a couple of dozen 2 pound+ shellcrackers by my house recently to smile and brag awhile. And for me to help clean. I asked, "How the heck do you do it, Duck?" He said, "I owe it all to my fairy dogmother." I asked, "Don't you mean 'godmother'?" He replied, "Obviously, you haven't seen her." Fortunately, our conversation was interrupted because my next question was going to be "Have you?" and I was afraid of the answer.

I know a lot of people who won't go fishing or hunting without their lucky charms (no, not the cereal), be they coins or caps or boxer shorts (no kidding!) or whatever. But I once went hunting with a fellow who wanted (and needed) his incantation. He insisted we stop by his uncle's house on the way to the woods. Uncle, it seems, was a full-blooded Cherokee and supposedly did an ancient ceremony that insured hunting success. We got to his house well before daylight and Uncle was sitting on the front porch answering owls. He seemed happy to perform the requested ceremony.

He made some hand signs that vaguely reminded me of a deaf/mute class I had once taken while murmuring a song that I think came from a 70's "Guess Who" album and blew pipe smoke into our faces for about 5 minutes. My friend got his buck that day, within about five minutes of our arrival. We hunted for a couple of more hours, but my eyes were still watering so bad from the pipe smoke, I couldn't see anything and we went home. So much for lucky invocations.

Like many things in life's little dramas, good luck and bad luck can swing like a saloon door. A while back I had a conversation with my friend Stinkin' Jenkins. We were talking quail hunting and lucky shots (most of the time those are one in the same) and he related the following to me. "The best shot I ever made in my life was when I dropped two birds at 50 paces with a .410 bolt action!"

"Wow, that was a lucky shot!"

He replied. "Yeah, but it took me a half hour to find the first one."

"Just bad luck you didn't get both."

"Oh, I did. I was just giving up and looked down and he was right at my feet."

"That was lucky!"

"You'd think so, but when I reached down to pick him up, I got snake bit right on my little finger."

"Aw, man, that was unlucky!"

"No sir! Turned out it was a black runner and not a rattler."

"Normally, it would have been, but the bite got infected, and I ended up in the hospital."

"Dang. Talk about bad luck."

"Actually, it wasn't. I struck up a romantic relationship with the nurse that was taking care of me."

"Now, that was lucky!"

"Not really, we got married."

I sensed that was the end of the conversation. Though, I couldn't help but recognize the coincidental wonder of the fact that the man got married because of a dead quail. I mean, what are the odds? Speaking of which, odds are involved with luck like barbeque sauce is involved with chicken. If you've ever taken your mortgage payment to a casino, you already know this, but the odds are never, ever, ever in your favor. I don't know the exact probability of hitting an inside straight, but I've been in enough deer camp poker games to know your chances of doing so are less than being trampled to death by a herd of whitetails.

"That storm's a long way to the west. It'll never get here before we get off the water."

"That little creek's not but three feet wide. I can jump it easy."

"Aw, Joe's old dog won't bite."

Wanna bet?

We normally apply "luck" to people or situations, but I am reluctantly inclined to believe, at the risk of being labeled a neolithic Druid, that certain "places" can be unlucky. I refer to a certain fishing resort and lodge in an adjoining state. I booked a two night stay there. I know the proprietor personally. He is as honest as a country preacher and assured me that the spotted bass were "jumping in the boats." When I arrived, the weather was perfect, the water was perfect and the outlook optimistic. Early the first morning, I met several fishermen at the dock who had been there the day before and asked all the right questions. How deep, what lure, what color, what presentation, what kind of cover? Which side of the lake? Wind direction? Sun or shade? Etc? Etc? Etc?

Now, I have seen a whole bunch of birthdays, and by the law of averages alone, I am a pretty good fisherman. But it was as if some great galactic predestination had occurred and by noon, I could hear the fishing gods giggling and snickering. By sunset, they were slapping their knees and roaring with laughter. Not a strike, not a bump, not a swirl, not even a hang up on a stump. When I returned to the dock that evening, I saw several limits of large, large fish. One was within 8 ounces of a state record. Perhaps, I thought, I was born under the wrong constellation. It certainly wasn't Pisces. After an extended deliberation with myself, I am convinced it was the "place."

If you have experienced this phenomenon, you probably cut your trip short and returned home in utter frustration. When you got there, perhaps the proprietor called you and told you to return immediately! Never in his life has he seen such a feeding frenzy! Take it from me. Don't do it. The state in which my bad luck lake is located makes my very favorite brown beverage in square bottles, but I wouldn't go back there for a case of the stuff.

Back before transistors were invented, my high school math teacher overheard a few of us wishing each other luck on the following day's exam. He proffered the idea that the more we studied, the luckier we would be. Of course, we didn't. We were in high school for gosh sakes. But teacher was absolutely right. It is not a good idea to depend upon luck for success, regardless of the circumstances. Remember the immortal words of Clint Eastwood. "You feeling lucky? Well, do ya Punk?" And we all know how that ended.

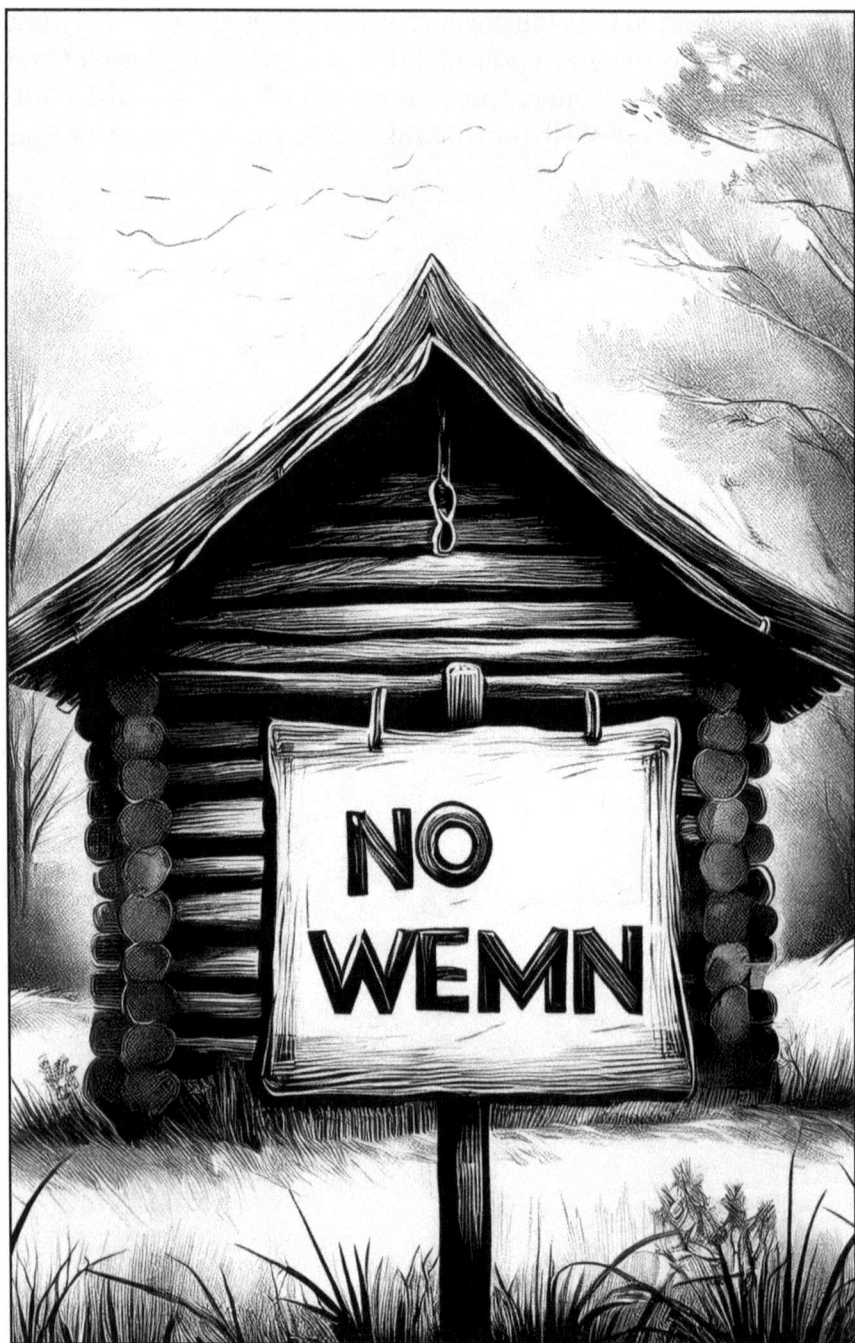

# 25.

# THE SPOUSE CONUNDRUM: FOR MEN ONLY

Recently, I made the ill-advised decision to point out to my wife Linda that one could not say her name without saying "duh." I know, I know, but alcohol was involved. And I knew immediately it was a mistake of epic proportions. The next morning, Ducky came by to pick me up to go fishing and I had gotten up late, probably because of the aforementioned alcohol. I asked Linda, "Honey, would you mind fixing a quick breakfast for us?" She replied, "Well, I would love to darling, but I'm too stupid to cook. Sorry." I didn't pursue the subject.

I told Ducky I would slap together a quick meal of toast and instant grits. He made a face and said he didn't like grits. I said, "Whaaaat? Of course, you like grits! You're a Southern boy!" He replied, "I know, but I ate enough grits as a kid to last a lifetime. I didn't even use toilet paper til I was 10. We used a whisk broom." At that, Linda broke up laughing. I said, "Ohhhh, I see. Ducky's funny. But I make a little harmless joke and lose my eating privileges." She replied, "Yeah, that pretty much covers it. I hate it when she does that. I said, "Listen Linda. About last night. I think I may have had a small stroke." For you younger guys out there, that's called an apology. We got bacon and eggs.

Now, I am sure some feminist twit, who disregarded the "For Men Only" in the title, is going to come screaming from her locker room about how I declared "a woman's place is in the kitchen."

Let me assure you madame, or whatever gender pronoun you proclaim to be these days, that my wife cooks because I cannot. The few times I have tried to make a meal in the kitchen, I have succeeded in ruining a very expensive frying pan, breaking the handles off of two boilers, denting the coffee pot and almost burning the house down. Therefore, I cook outside, on the grill, as God intended men to do.

I'm sure I've told you before, but Ducky has had more wives than an Old Testament king. Not all at once though. Unlike Ducky, I made sure Linda liked to fish and tolerated hunting before I ever popped the question. Ducky just wandered into his marriages blindly, with no forethought about the really important things in life. And he has paid the price. One marriage lasted less than a week because she thought she had lost her wedding ring and found out he had pawned it when a really beautiful Bernelli went on sale. You can't make this stuff up.

That wasn't the last time sporting goods got him into trouble. He once told one of his less mathematically inclined mates that he had bought a bass boat, but it only cost three thousand ninety-two hundred and eight dollars. She said that sounded reasonable until one of her more intellectual friends pointed out that it was $12,208. I think that was the same wife who asked him if he knew he had run over a deer when he came home with a newly harvested buck strapped to the hood of his truck. She was stupid on so many levels.

Ducky had some doozies. He once got a divorce arguing about how much they had paid for their wedding bands. But most of his marital failures have revolved around the fact that his brides had nothing in common with his sporting pursuits. One thought "the great outdoors" was an unscreened porch. He took another on her first bass fishing trip and instead of using the Zebco 202 he had brought for her, she picked up his top-of-the-line Quantum reel and Ugly Stick rod and cast into the lake. The whole thing. Line, lure, rod and reel. Into 40 feet of water. I once asked him how he picked 'em. He said, "Just lucky I guess."

Not that Ducky ever tried. We once came home very, very late from a deer hunting trip, due to a stopover at a nearby tavern on the way back and Ducky's wife was absolutely beside herself with worry and anger and relief that we had shown up at all. She came running onto the carport in a frenzy of incoherent babbling and tears as she tried to vent all of her feelings at once. Ducky stopped dead in his tracks, put his hands on both her shoulders, looked her squarely in the eye and said, "What's that girl? Timmy's in the well?" I fell out. Couldn't help it. Had that been my wife, the following conversation would have later ensued. Detective: "Have you identified the victims, Sergeant?" Sergeant: "No sir. They were too badly beaten."

Our friend, Stinkin' Jenkins, the area's unofficial catfish bait production champion, has the ideal fisherman's wife. Now, she's not much to look at. Jenkins once accused her of lying through both teeth. And our crowd is big on get-togethers for cook-outs for various game species and her house is not a popular destination on the entertainment circuit. She decorated her living room around a bean bag chair and has two bug zappers hanging in the kitchen. And most of her coffee cups advertise bail bondsmen. And she is not especially bright. Several of us were once discussing the jungle warfare going on in Central America between the government and rebel forces and she asked, "How do you reckon they teach them gorillas to fight?" Jenkins just hung his head and walked off. However, she can not only clean a big blue before the truck is unloaded, but fry it fit for a Wesson Oil commercial. Jenkins is smart enough to know he better hang on to her, because she is one of the few well-fed women in this hemisphere that would put up with him or his stench.

One of our other friends, whom we will call John and who will otherwise remain nameless for reasons that will soon become apparent, has a wife who is a pain, both physically and mentally. At a cookout in their backyard one evening, John was dipping crappie filets in the batter and dropping them into a kettle of boiling oil, when his wife rushed up out of nowhere in a frantic attempt to correct his method of either dipping or dropping and managed to push him against said kettle which violently splashed boiling oil onto several of us, mostly me.

I have, in my long life, fallen from a pier I was repairing during a lake drawdown and landed on a concrete block. On my knee cap. I have had a fellow hunter following behind me jump a ditch, slip and break off his front teeth in the back of my skull. I have had several #9 dove shot removed from my calf in the field by a retired, shaky, nearsighted doctor with a pocketknife. Without anesthetic. I have been bitten by a large, stubborn bowfin that had to be pried from my fingers with two pair of pliers. If all of that pain were molded together into one excruciating ball, it would not equal having several layers of skin suddenly removed by boiling oil.

I think the psychological term that applies to John's wife's uncontrollable urge to take over his cooking chore is called the I Can Do Everything Better Than You Syndrome. The key word there is "everything." So, when they go fishing together and she catches the biggest fish, she brags. Relentlessly. When he catches the biggest, she tells him what he did wrong to keep her from catching it. Endlessly. He stays with her because her parents are filthy rich and very old.

Since my wife sometimes reads this drivel I write, I would like to add that I hope your spouse is as compatible with your sports pursuits as is mine. She is the perfect combination of support, enthusiasm and participation. Rarely a complaint, always a smile. (See what I did there?) And in the interest of fairness, I was going to write a follow-up column with the same title except "For Women Only." However, for the life of me, I cannot come up with any viable faults or criticisms or complaints that would apply to men. I'll keep trying.

# 26.

# STUPID IS AS STUPID DOES

I was reading an article the other day that absolutely depressed me. Back in the late 1940's, the Zero Hour Bomb Company made explosives to start oil flowing on the oil rigs of Oklahoma. Their patents were expiring, and they needed to diversify in order to stay in business. Along came an inventor who offered an alternative to the baitcasting reel that would not backlash, and the company picked it up and gave the world the Zebco 33. Now, I knew all that. What I didn't know was where he got his idea.

Seems he was in a meat market and noticed that the twine they used in packaging did not come from a revolving spool, but from a stationary one attached to the wall. Now, it occurred to me that I do not know how to set the timer on my dryer and this guy came up with an idea that revolutionized fishing over 70 years ago by walking into a meat market. I could have spent several days and nights in that place and never, ever, ever have thought of such a thing.

Summertime and the livin' is easy and the day after my epiphany, Ducky and I were sitting on my deck late in the afternoon enjoying the results of some refiner's hard work at a Kentucky distillery. I told him I was as dumb as a 'No Dogs Allowed' sign at an Institute for the Blind and related the story of the Zebco 33 and how the inventor got the idea and how stupid that made me feel. He told me I should not give it a second thought because he had always known how stupid I was.

I took great exception to that statement and retorted with "O.K., Einstein, how does a radio work?" He shrugged his shoulders and said, "Simple. It's magic. The radio itself, theoretically, is full of elves and leprechauns and...." I interrupted, "Alright, bar is closed," screwed the cap back on the bottle and set it behind my chair. "Seriously, Duck, doesn't finding out stuff like that make you feel stupid?"

He took his glasses off, put the end of one earpiece in the corner of his mouth and stared off into the distance. He actually looked intelligent there for a second. For a second. Then he said, "No, I feel stupid when I drive my boat 10 miles up the lake to my favorite fishing hole, raise the outboard, put down my trolling motor, work my way to the back of the cove and discover I left both my rods in the truck."

"You didn't," I said.

"Fraid so. And then I ran out of gas on the way back."

"Ducky, that's really dumb."

He wasn't through. "And I forgot to recharge my battery the night before and couldn't use my trolling motor, so I sat in the middle of the lake most of the afternoon before a Marine Police boat spotted me."

"Ducky, that's not stupidity, it's senility. Stupidity is when you tell your fellow competitors where you caught that limit of huge bass. And there's a full day left in the tournament. Stupidity is when you tell a game warden he looks like an alligator gar. Stupidity is when you ask your mother-in-law not to tell your wife about your new $3,000 shotgun."

"Well, I'm glad to know I'm just forgetful, not ignorant."

"No, no, no. Ignorance is something else entirely. The root word of ignorance is ignore. It means you know the truth but simply choose to disregard it. Like most politicians. Stupidity and senility can be excused. Ignorance can't."

"So, when we were kids and headed out fishing that day and I almost killed myself racing y'all on Dead Man's Hill when my bike fell apart and my Dad called me ignorant, he was wrong?"

"Indeed, he was. You were just stupid."

"I'm glad to hear that."

"I know you are."

Ducky then related a few risqué stories of girls he had dated in college that we can't print in a family publication, and we analyzed, since they were too young to be senile, whether they were stupid or ignorant. Most, we determined, turned out to be neither. They were brainless. Especially since they had been dating Ducky. After that little discussion, Ducky slid his empty glass across the patio table and said, "I'll drink to that" and I retrieved the bottle from behind my chair.

"Last one, Duck. Remember, we've got to get up early in the morning for that drive to Lake Eufaula. Besides, you don't want to turn into Uncle Romer."

"Who?"

"My Uncle Romer. He used to get plastered every Friday night. Needless to say, that severely perturbed my Aunt Louise. One Friday he came home late and wanting to get sympathy rather than the usual tirade from her, he fell onto the living room floor and moaned, 'Louise, honey, I think I'm dying. Please, darling, pray for me'. Louise, knowing full well he was drunk as a skunk, but feigning concern, dropped to her knees, clasped her hands under her chin and said, 'Lord, please help my poor old drunk husband'. Uncle Romer sat straight upright and said, 'Dang, Louise, don't tell Him I'm drunk!'" Ducky said, "Last one."

The next day we were on Eufaula worm fishing the points. It was hot. I mean sweltering hot. And we weren't having any luck. Ducky suggested we try easing back into the winding creek beside the point we were fishing and I quickly agreed. He pointed us there with the bow-mounted trolling motor and when we hit the shade of the overhanging trees, it was absolutely delightful. We hadn't gone 20 yards before we each picked up a yearling. Encouraged, we moved even deeper into the narrowing creek, enjoying the occasional strike and the canopy of coolness above us. Eventually it got so narrow that there was only a few feet between the boat and the bank on each side and the limbs were getting lower and as I was making one final cast, my worm wrapped around a twig and got hung. That was the first time I had looked up. I wish I hadn't.

You have probably heard the song "Black Water Hattie" with the line "And the snakes hang thick from the cypress trees like sausage on the smoke house wall." I am convinced Patrick Simmons was sitting in a bass boat in that very creek when he penned that verse. I said quietly, "Duck." Without looking back at me, he replied, "Yeah?" I said, "No Ducky, I mean duck. And back us the hell out of here." He turned and looked at me then, following my gaze upward and his eyes got as big as some of those reptilian heads staring back down at us.

Ducky's mouth began moving but nothing came out. I slowly got out my pocketknife and cut the line attached to my hung-up worm at the reel, not daring to stand up or even reach up to free it. I am not mathematically proficient enough to even calculate the number of snakes in those trees. The closest I can come is lots and lots and lots and lots. We scrunched our shoulders, getting as small as we could, waiting for, nay, expecting one or more to fall on us at any moment. Ducky began to slowly reverse our route. He was muttering, almost incoherently, a constant mantra to the trolling motor and battery, "Please don't quit, please don't quit, please don't quit." I think he threw an "I love you" in there a few times.

Given my proclivity for fear of snakes, I am actually surprised I did not just divorce myself from the real world and go clinically insane. I think the only thing that saved me was the fact I did not look up again. After one or two Biblical eternities, the creek widened enough that Ducky was able to turn the boat around facing back toward the lake. He jerked the trolling motor up, made a single bound to the steering console, fired up the outboard and gunned it. We left that creek into open water like we were fired out of a slingshot. We didn't stop until we reached the landing.

As we loaded the boat on the trailer and stashed our gear in the truck bed, not a word was spoken. I think it's called traumatic verbal paralysis. We then climbed into the cab and still sat silent for a while. Finally, I said, in a voice still noticeably shaky, "Well, I can now predict the future. I know what my next nightmare will be about." Ducky countered with, " I learned a lot about myself today. I know I am not senile enough to ever forget that place. I know I am not ignorant enough to overlook it. And I know I am not stupid enough to ever go back there again."

# 27.

# BIG CITY CRITTERS

I heard an idiot, probably a PETA representative, on television the other day reprimanding we uneducated morons for the decline in animal populations. He said it was due to the encroachment of mankind's evil civilization. Of course, he did so without a scintilla of evidence, documentation, data or statistics. Tree-huggers are laboring under the delusion, like many of today's politicians, that whatever falls out of their mouths is truth simply because they said it. As for me, I dispute the very premise that animal populations are declining at all and that if there is a positive or negative flux, available habitat has nothing to do with it.

Remember, these are the same people who were screeching hysterically about the disappearing polar bears. Turns out, there are more than there have ever been. And gray wolves. Ask the cattlemen about that. And several years ago, they imagined that the alligator was almost non-existent and somehow had them placed on the endangered species list. At that time, there were several ponds I would not fish on foot for fear of being gator et. During that period when this animal was "endangered," this fellow invited me to a large oxbow lake off of the Alabama River to bass fish from his jon boat. I met him there shortly before dawn one morning and we stood on the tiny pier before launching and he said, "Watch this."

Now, I had lived just long enough to know that when somebody said, "Watch this," as likely as not, something unpleasant was going to follow. He shined his Maglite out across the water and there were so many pairs of red eyes, it looked as if the surface was on fire. "What's the biggest one you've seen in here?" I inquired calmly and scientifically. He studied a moment and said, "Well, the boat's twelve foot and I've seen half a dozen bigger'n it." I went home. Endangered, my big ol' butt.

I am of the opinion that most all native species, including game animals, are encroaching on our habitat, not the other way around. Having had the opportunity in my long life to live in a wide variety of domiciles, in a wide variety of settings, including deep country, small community, little town and big city, I can attest that deer, squirrel, rabbit, fox, coyote, turkey, dove, quail, bobcat, coon, boar, bear and many other species of wildlife and game not only live, but thrive among we despicable humans. Out in the country, I have had each of the species listed above in my yard at one time or another and have harvested and eaten several from there, most notably whitetail and turkey. Closer to where the multitudes congregate, most still join us and do so in abundance.

For instance, the little too-closely-packed subdivision in the large city to which I retired to live out my days is simply alive with certain species. There are more doves living on my block than the entirety of flocks on the best shooting fields I have ever visited. In season, my wife keeps a close eye on me in case I make a break for the gun cabinet. And just yesterday, I had my coffee watching two cottontails munching on some kind of weed on the lawn I promised her I would cut last week. Fishing got in the way.

Our personal family squirrel, Rocky (If you are old enough to remember Bullwinkle cartoons, you know where we got the name) uses our porch rail as his banquet hall. The dining format is BYOP (Bring Your Own Pecan). The other evening, Linda and I were sitting on the porch, quietly reading in the dying light, when Rocky nonchalantly walked out from under my chair into my line of sight. Not being able to immediately recognize what had unexpectedly appeared between my feet, I jumped (almost imperceptibly of course), which in turn caused Rocky to realize he was not alone, switch into high gear, climb the table and hurl himself onto the corner post, just inches from my wife's face. All in approximately two seconds.

There was a scream. It may have been Rocky, though I've never known a squirrel to emit that particular sound, so l assume it was my wife. She, on the other hand, has this silly notion that it was.... well, it's too ridiculous to repeat. The incident shook Rocky so badly that he did not come back to dine for a couple of days. And I took to moving my chair up against the wall so it could not be approached from the rear.

There is nothing in my neighborhood proper that could be classified as big game. I haven't seen any wild pigs, with the possible exception of a rather rotund and unfortunately unattractive lady down the street. She does have warts. And one of her tusks is broken off. But I don't think she would qualify anyway. And the only turkey I've seen is this pencil-necked kid who lives on the next street and jogs around the block on weekends. He wears an outfit that had to have been featured in a Broadway musical. I'll give him this. He is the only person I have ever seen that could run, sing along with his earphones, read and text without falling down or getting run over. There are tons of chipmunks around. Though not classified as a game animal, I suppose when the Apocalypse or another Great Depression comes, they could keep us alive for a while. And I hear they taste pretty good. Ducky told me that. I didn't ask how he knew. The lady across the street was worried about them burrowing beneath her trees and killing the root systems, so she put out a bunch of ceramic garden gnomes to keep them away. I don't know about the chipmunks, but they keep me away. I don't like garden gnomes. Or circus clowns. They both give me the willies. I can just picture a lot of you out there nodding in agreement. You know who you are. Surprisingly, rodeo clowns don't bother me. Especially since they call themselves bullfighters nowadays. But I digress. Editors don't like that much, but it's a hobby of mine.

Anyway, I have seen beaucoup deer in the undeveloped acreage adjoining the bypass which runs by our subdivision. Especially in the headlights at night. Some big racks too. Late at night, I can sit on the porch and listen to the coyotes call from that same vicinity. The dogs in the neighborhood try to answer them. They fail miserably. And occasionally, coons get into the garbage cans and possum eat from the dog food dish out back.

I had a run-in with a particularly vicious possum one night recently. I had gone out back for some obscure reason elderly minds can't ever recall and he was raiding Spot's bowl. He saw me and beat a hasty retreat. Then he stopped and turned to glare at me with those beady little eyes. I picked up a rock from the flower bed and nailed him pretty good. He fell over "dead" as they are wont to do, but when I took a step toward him, he stood up, showed his rather large and sharp teeth, hissed and charged. Then I beat a hasty retreat. I hate possums almost as much as garden gnomes and circus clowns.

The only black bears I have ever seen were years ago when I lived so far out in the boonies, I got Christmas cards in February. You may see one if you live on a dirt county road. I live on a paved street named after a flower. If I see one here, I will check myself into the nearest mental health facility.

Since I no longer reside near my favorite hunting haunts, resulting in long debilitating drives and since I have been afflicted with that insidious little disease known as "old age," and cannot walk very far anymore, my wife, in an attempt to assuage my frustrations, bought me one of those little plastic guns that shoots salt and kills bugs. She thought it might appease my hunting instincts. It wasn't a bad idea. I don't have to go anywhere. I can sit on my porch and still hunt. Even make short stalks.

Of course, my prey is houseflies, mosquitoes, moths, spiders, and the like, but on the other hand, there is no closed season and the ammo is, well, cheap salt. The only major drawback is that the weapon only has a killing range of three feet. And there isn't a lot of big game. I did knock one of those little green lizards off the steps the other day, so I suppose that's something.

However, if you are thinking about getting one, let me warn you. Do not try to bring down a wasp with it. It just pisses them off really, really bad. They will come after you, full of vengeance, stinger first. Last week, I had to grab my gun by the barrel and fend one off swinging the stock. It isn't exactly the challenge of a charging, wounded boar, but it was nonetheless exhilarating. The other drawback about bug hunting is you can't eat what you kill. At least I don't think so. I'll ask Ducky.

Back to the real game. The next time you hear someone from the "woke culture" complaining about loss of animal habitat due to human incursion, please tell them to shut up and go back to sleep. But I must admit. I haven't seen an alligator on my street. Yet.

# 28.

# FISHING ETIQUETTE

It's not just for tea parties and cotillions. Good manners also apply to the participants in the time-honored sport of fishing. The practices at black tie gatherings and formal dinner parties should be applied to us. Conforming to these social traditions could not only prevent undue embarrassment but enhance your reputation and even save you money.

Emily Post, one of the queens of etiquette, absolutely prohibits bragging in polite society. Now, since that particular characteristic is built into the DNA of fishermen, bragging is an extremely difficult habit to overcome but remember this: Just because you have a half-dozen engraved plaques, Snoopy statues and assorted drinking vessels given to you by your grandchildren that say "World's Greatest Fishermen" does not make you the world's greatest fisherman. And there are plenty of folks out there who are going to be willing to point that out in front of your red face.

A close cousin of braggartry is loud talking, which Ms. Post deems garish and completely unacceptable. I, for one, agree. On the water, it is indeed bad manners when someone talks so blaringly loud that folks on the other side of the lake can hear you. It is irritating. You don't have to whisper like you're giving away honey hole secrets. And Mike Iconelli, I realize you are a talented pro, but to paraphrase Tom Hanks, "There's no screaming in bass fishing!" Someday he's going to do that and every TV camera within range is going to focus on him and film as he lands a 12-pound foul hooked gar. Bet he won't scream anymore. Who am I kidding?

And there can be serious consequences to ignoring the voice volume rule. You are at your favorite boat ramp and remember, "Dang Joe! I forgot my fishing license! Oh, well." Now, sound carries over water at something like four times the distance and speed it does over land and there's a game warden idling in the cove next to the ramp. He is going to be filling out the ticket with everything but your name and address while he watches you and Joe go directly across the lake and cut your outboard. When you put down your trolling motor and make your first cast, he is going to be on you like a duck on a June Bug.

Akin to loud talking on etiquette's forbidden list is profanity or obscenity in the presence of ladies. Let me modify that to include "in the presence of anyone you do not know." A while back, I was doing my civic duty by participating in a fishing rodeo at a local pond, put on by the Boy Scouts as a fund-raising event. As I was unhooking a yearling bass, I drove a #4 worm hook up under my thumb nail. Before I made a sound, I looked furtively up and down the bank to make sure no kids were nearby. There was only an older gentleman standing about 20 feet away, so I said, as quietly as I could, "Mx#@@*#effenC+@^>#@xSx@%l!!" as I removed the hook. My string of expletives would have made a drill sergeant blush. The fellow down the bank asked if I was O.K. I replied, "Yeah, sorry about that. I hope you're not a preacher or anything." "Monsignor," he corrected. "Our Lady of Eternal Life." It was only then that I noticed his collar. I said to myself (so I thought) "Oh, Good Lord." He said, "I'm glad to see that you pray, my son." I quickly departed and left a hefty donation with the Scout Master at the gate. A sort of penitence I guess. The embarrassment was bad enough, but the incidence left me with psychological scars. To this day, when I see a priest, my thumb hurts.

Behavior around the ladies seems to be of high priority among the social elite. We are told by those who are concerned with such that gentlemen should never partake in the use of tobacco products when the weaker sex is present. (For those politically correct people out there, their words, not mine.) Hence, when the dinner party ends, the men are to retire to the study or library to smoke and have a glass of $90 per pint brandy. Now, my buddies and I, much like you and yours I'm sure, don't have formal dinner parties nor serve $90 liquor. We do on occasion have wine and it is served from only the best boxes. And we don't own enough books to fill a half shelf in a study or library. Hell, I don't even think Jenkins is functionally literate and the rest of our crowd's reading material consists of a few stacks of outdoor magazines. But we are civilized enough to know that most womenfolk don't care for smoke.

So, when a rain shower ran us inside at Ducky's last barbeque, we went to the porch afterwards to light up and have a cold beer or, in my case, to have a chaw and a cold beer. Ducky's wife at the time was a cat person and the damn thing ran up the steps and headed toward the back door where she was standing, looking through the glass slider. Without thinking, given my innate disapproval of felines, I let loose a stream of Red Man that caught the Siamese squarely on the side of its head. Most of the men on the porch broke out in soft applause and nods of approval. She gagged and passed out. The wife, not the cat. She was not seen the rest of the day. The cat, not the wife. She filed for divorce the following day. The wife, not the cat. The day after that, I received a brand-new Mitchell ultra-light open face from Ducky through the mail. Which brings us to the rules of etiquette regarding Thank You notes and gifts.

But such communiques, as well as the subjects of punctuality, cell phone use and clothing fashion are rarely applicable to fishermen. Being on time is of no concern to us when fishing and food are involved. We'll be there! And some of us don't even own a cell phone and still have an old rotary dial at home. As far as fashion design, the primary business, casual and sports attire of fishermen consists of some combination of jeans, camouflage shirts and jackets and boots or sneakers. And baseball caps. I wore a tie once. Didn't like it much. Ducky is the only exception I have ever seen.

One weekend in September, he walked into a grocery store, looked down and realized he had on white tennis shoes. Two weeks after Labor Day! He left immediately. It was the fashion faux pas of the season. The horror! But, as you know, Ducky's strange.

A great number of Miss Manner's regulations deal with dining. Since most of our dining experiences take place in the back yard or around a campfire, we have to modify them somewhat. For instance, "Wait to eat before the host is seated (on the beer cooler)" and "The shortest (plastic) fork should be placed to the far right of the (paper) plate" and "It is of utmost importance that all utensils (fingers) be spotless (including spatulas and tongs)" and "Never floss your teeth (if you have any) at the table."

Personal interactions are often noted in the rules, and they tell us to refrain from both the "weak and clammy" handshake and the "bonecrusher" handshake. This suggestion is useless to us. No fisherman I have ever known would dare offer anyone a "weak and clammy" hand. Instant banishment. Not only from the group, but possibly the town. We always opt for the "bonecrusher." Our rule is, "The handshake ends when one participant is on at least one knee."

Finally, those who know of such things warn us; in order to be accepted by polite society, we must put a stress on remembering names. Listen, this isn't applicable either. Whether or not we remember someone's name, we most often address them "Hey you old butthead!" anyway. So, dear authors of etiquette books and columns, if we ever meet, do not be offended if I say the same to you.

# 29.

# STUFF FISHERMEN SHOULDN'T DO

There are literally thousands of sources from which to learn about what fishermen should do to be successful, including the tactical, technical, and legal. But there are none about what you should not do. Until now. Garnered from decades of personal experience, these guidelines may prevent embarrassment, frustration, and even personal injury as you pursue your favorite sport.

Under no circumstances should you argue with an irate landowner. You are ultralight fishing a beautiful little creek meandering through acres of mature hardwoods. You hear a shuffling in the leaves behind you and turn to find a frowning man. "Jest whut do ya think yore doin' boy?" You explain that you are fishing a stream on state land. "My great granddaddy bought this hyar prop'ty back in nine-teen hunnert 'n ought eight. He didn't 'low no fishin' on it an' I don't neither. Git yore butt often it!" Now, you may have a GPS in your pocket that proves it is state land, and he is wrong as a U-turn. But he doesn't know what a GPS is and you can bet your lucky silver dollar that he has a 45-hog leg stuffed in the side pocket of his overalls. Do not make eye contact, say "Yessir," turn and walk back the way you came. If you hear a metallic click, drop everything you have and run. Do not look back. Do not go back. Ever.

Never fish in a standing position from a 10-foot aluminum jon boat. You are going to fall overboard. Maybe not this time. Maybe not next time. But eventually. And this should be supplemented by a secondary fact. It is impossible for a full-grown man to reenter a

10-foot aluminum jon boat from the water. If you are alone, hang on to the side of the boat and swim it back to shore. If you have a partner, wait until he stops laughing his tail off and have him paddle you back to shore. At that time, you can remove the top-water bait, which was initially hung on a shallow stump until you jerked too hard but is now firmly implanted in your forehead. A tetanus shot will be required.

Do not consume alcoholic beverages and fish simultaneously. These are two different sports. It's like trying to play golf and deer hunt at the same time. It just doesn't work. I woke up one morning with a real bad hangover, stitches in my left ear, a really expensive worm rod broken into three pieces and a missing trolling motor. Oh yeah, there were a series of pictures on my cell phone, each sequentially closer than the last, of a really pretty bikini clad lady obviously sunning herself on the end of a private pier. And in each photo, she seemed to be increasingly more angry. The last few shots are only a blur. Much like my memory.

If anyone asks you to go "noodling," politely decline the invitation. For those of you who think this is Italian food preparation, let me explain. Noodling is a method of catching catfish by wading into a lake or river and blindly sticking your hands and arms into holes under the bank and letting the fish bite down on said hands and arms, whereby you are supposed to retrieve them. In this process, there is a high likelihood that you will be severely injured or die. You may have your fingers removed by a snapping turtle, be bitten by a moccasin, or be drug under and drowned by a 60-pound flathead. This "sport" is, what's the phrase I'm looking for....oh yeah, completely insane. However, If I'm ever in a bar fight, I want a noodler on my side.

Finally, if you ever remove a limb blocking the logging road you're on, make sure it isn't covered with a poison ivy vine before you step into the woods and take a leak. You will only make this mistake once in your life.

For those of you who have yet to experience these situations, good luck. As for me, I'm an old man. Nothing else could possibly happen.

# 30.

# THE DARK SIDE

When I look back to my days as a younger man, I am appalled at how stupid I was. I am surprised I could dress myself. I actually used to fish at night! It was as if I occasionally took temporary leave of my mental faculties. I never hunted at night. When most sportsmen think about hunting after dark, two things come to mind. Spotlighting deer and slogging around a swamp after coons.

The first is not only illegal, but despicable. And I will not give that activity any further notoriety by discussing it other than to say its participants, in the words of my grandmother, should be stripped naked, tied behind Pa's tractor and drug around courthouse square. (Bless her heart, granny could be a vicious old woman.)

The second, coon hunting, doesn't require a great deal of discussion either, except to say its adherents suffer from mental illness. And I don't like to speak ill of the mentally ill. There but for the grace of God go I.

Back to the stupidity of night fishing. The level of imbecility of this activity can be measured almost completely by one thing. Location. For instance, as a young man, I spent the night catfishing on the river with a couple of buddies. We set up camp on a sandbar berm exposed due to the low water level about 30 yards from the normal bank and about the same distance from the river. We spent the night tending the campfire, telling stories and walking down to the water to check our rod sets. By 2 a.m., we had a nice string of blues and channels. We did a final rebait, set our lines back out and turned in. Looking back, we should have paid some heed to the ominous thunder to the north of us.

At first light, we awoke to find ourselves on a tiny island. The rods, reels, fish, minnow buckets and campfire were all gone. So was our composure. I cannot come up with an adjective that describes the panic that set in. "Unspeakable" and "Incomprehensible" come to mind. There was a lot of screeching and running around in a very small circle. We ended up half-wading, half-swimming back to the shore in a life-threatening current. Unless you catch a world record bass, a fishing trip should never end with you on your knees in intense prayers of gratitude.

Boat fishing the lake at night isn't much better, except you can be fairly sure the lake isn't going to rise rapidly. But fishing the lake after dark is a slow and tedious process. You will only drive your boat at daylight speed until you hit a half-submerged log. Thereafter, you will move at idle speed only. The last time I participated in this idiocy, I was fishing piers with lights on the end of them. This one particular little dock had a long-curved aluminum pole, and an old streetlamp cover over the light. On my second cast, the lure and line wrapped tightly around the pole.

I began jerking it, easily at first, but with increasing force as frustration set in. I did not want to approach it and scare away any bass lurking there. As I jerked harder, though, the pole began to bang against the pier. There was a cabin about 20 yards up the bank and I saw a guy look cautiously out of a window. He could not see me in the dark but could see his light whipping about for no apparent reason. I assume he thought his dock was being attacked by poltergeists. He walked out of the door brandishing a shotgun.

I cut my line off at the reel, hit the trolling motor and started off down the lake. That's when he fired, and I saw the pier light explode. I have always wondered if he thought buckshot would kill ghosts or if he thought the light was the victim of demonic possession and he just wanted to put it out of its misery. I never returned to ask.

The worst possible form of night fishing is on a farm pond. Unless you have been blindfolded, sealed in a barrel and placed at the bottom of Carlsbad Caverns, you have no idea how dark an isolated farm pond can be on a cloudy, moonless night. My friend Ducky Jones talked me into going topwater bass fishing one summer evening. He came to the house to pick me up.

On the way, I asked him if he had flashlights. He said, "Oh, nooooo. You can't use flashlights out there. They scare the bass! And they might disturb the bulls." Before I could ask the obvious, he asked if I had brought a motorcycle helmet. "Why ever would I need a motorcycle helmet?" He explained that you can't see where your lure is, you don't know how much line you have out, and when you set the hook on a strike and miss, the lure will be coming back at you with the approximate speed of a major league fast pitch. He added that his helmet had a full-face shield.

I was several questions behind by this time. "With no flashlights, how are we going to look in the tackle box to change lures?" He said, "Sense of touch." I continued, "How are we going to see where we're walking?" He said, "Sense of smell." I thought for a moment he had experienced a stroke, but he laughed and told me to stay close to him. I said, "Bulls?" He said, "Don't worry, it's not that bad." He was wrong.

After we arrived and started fishing, my questions continued.

"What was that?"

"Where are you?"

"What was that?"

"Are you behind me?"

"What was that?"

"Did I just cast into the pasture?"

"How can you hear in that helmet?"

"Did you just say 'stake' or 'snake'?"

"What bats?"

"When are they going to start biting?"

"What the hell was that?"

"Will you take me home now?"

"Please?"

# 31.


# MORE SNAKE STUFF

What an unimaginative title. I have probably told you before about my fear of snakes (called ophidiophobia for those of you who are scientifically inclined). Have you ever noticed that "phobia" implies that the condition is associated with negative connotations? I personally think ophidiophobia should be included on any checklist indicating good mental health. Empathy? Check. Self-control? Check. Ophidiophobia? Check. Sane person. Anyway, here are some more of my misadventures with them. Hence, the horrible title.

There are three kinds of people in the world. Those who are petrified of snakes; those who are petrified of snakes and won't admit it; those who are too stupid to be petrified of snakes. My friend Ducky Jones belongs to the second group. He does admit he has a "healthy regard" for them. When we were about 10 years old, Ducky and I were walking in the woodlot behind my house, when we came upon a Diamondback, coiled and rattling a few feet from us. I froze, in unspeakable horror, and did not move until it slithered off. When it finally left, Ducky was gone.

I heard a voice from above that asked, "Are you alright?" I assumed it was the Guardian Angel who had been watching over me during the incident. But when flakes of bark began floating down around me, I realized it was Ducky. He was in the very tip top of a 30-foot pine, hanging on for dear life. I thought we would have to get a fire truck to retrieve him. But he managed to climb part of the way down and fall the rest of the way. It is providential that young bones are flexible. "Healthy regard," indeed.

As for the third group, I do not trust them. Now, there are many people I don't trust. I don't trust people who smile all the time, who won't take a shot of Kentucky bourbon, or who have had more than 5 shots of Kentucky bourbon. Which brings us back to people who smile all the time. And I don't trust people who do not have enough sense to be afraid of snakes. There is something wrong with them.

With the exception of ex-wives and Yankees, Ducky, on the other hand, seems to trust most everyone. So, imagine my surprise when he told me recently that he had turned down a dream all-expenses-paid trip to the Gulf one weekend because he didn't have confidence in the fellow who made the offer. I asked him why and he told me the guy's name was Bubba.

"So?" I queried. He explained that people with that name could not be depended upon. "'Bubba' is a mispronunciation of 'brother'," he patiently professed. "It was a name given by a younger sibling who could not pronounce 'brother'. Anyone who could go through life with a nickname given to him by a mentally undeveloped, illiterate, speech impaired baby is not mentally stable. It's cute at 4. It isn't at 40."

I could come closer to explaining the nuances of nuclear fission than the way Ducky's brain works. I could have asked him about being nicknamed after the vocalizations of a waterfowl, but thought better of it, because he knows the aliases I had as a kid. Since most of them dealt with bodily functions, I chose not to broach the subject.

Back to snakes. My reaction when spotting one usually falls into two categories: Rigid immobilization or rapid flight. And though I am also rendered mute, that has rarely affected my ability to run. Several times, I have been walking with a group of hunters going to a blind or dove field and someone would ask, "Where's Garry?" Someone who knows me well would reply, "Watch your step."

Now, I understand my fear might be classified as irrational. And that's O.K. I understand there are levels of trepidation. I always remind people who scoff at me that it wasn't a hippopotamus that gave an apple to Eve. Some people may not react as I do, but I have been that way all my life. I once breathlessly told my Uncle of one of the leviathans I had seen down by the creek.

Holding out my arms as far as I could, I gasped, "Snake!" He asked, "What kind was it?" I replied, "Snake!" He said, "O.K., where was it?" Still standing with my arms spread, I replied, "Snake!" He asked, "O.K., what color was it?" I replied, "Snake!" He said, "I see." No, he didn't.

They are evil, regardless of make or model. There was a little poem they used when I was a kid to identify the difference between a Coral and a Crimson King snake. Since both have bands of yellow, red and black, the poem read, "Red on yellow, hurt a fellow. Red on black, friend of Jack." I revised it to fit my disposition. "Red on yellow, turn to jello. Red on black, heart attack"

My fear of the vile reptiles has occasionally been beneficial. When I was 13 or so, the neighborhood bully, much older and larger than me (as bullies tend to be), threw a dead 4-foot garter snake at me as I rode my bike in front of his house. Such was my terror that I became inexplicably and suddenly enraged and lost whatever sanity a 13-year-old can have.

I dropped my bike in the middle of the street and lit into him like a starving bobcat on a rabbit. There was lots of screeching during my attack and to this day I don't know which one of us it was. When they pulled me off of him, he looked like he had fallen out of a tree, hit every branch on the way down and landed in a barrel of cheese graters. But he never bothered me again.

That's not the last time I witnessed such a reaction. One Spring Saturday, an old Army buddy called and told me the bream were bedding in his farm pond. I grabbed my fly rod and was there in half an hour. He was out on his tractor plowing under last year's corn field and I walked to the edge of the tract. He held up a couple of fingers indicating he would be two more minutes.

As I watched his work, a huge snake, obviously irritated at having been run over, tried to climb the moving tractor and eat him. It fell off. It tried again. Randall pulled out a .45 auto to defend himself and promptly blew a hole in an $800 tractor tire. This so infuriated him that he shut off the machine, jumped down and hollered, "Ground moccasin! Where is he?"

Now, I had never heard the term "Ground moccasin" before or since. I suppose it was a local term, but I do know it was poisonous, regardless of its light color, because I had seen perfectly its triangular head outlined against the soon-to-be-flat tire. Now, the only adjective that should precede moccasin is "dead" and the only phrase that should describe its proximity is "way over yonder."

But here Randall was wading around in dead, broken corn stalks looking for a monstrous snake the color of dead, broken corn stalks. With a pistol! In those days we could both hit a silhouette at 300 meters with an M-16, but neither of us could hit a fence post at 5 feet with a sidearm. At this point, I was considering my friend had experienced a complete mental breakdown and I began slowly backing away, getting ready to sprint for my truck.

Then, he suddenly emptied his clip into the ground a couple of feet in front of him and yelled "Got 'im!" He then slowly walked toward me. I restrained myself from running because the crazy man's gun was empty. When he came up to me, he was the color of a boiled, hairless cat. His knees gave way, and he sat down in place, shaking. It was then I knew he realized his anger had caused him to lapse into a fit of stupidity.

I know because he said, "Man, that was stupid." It is difficult to console anyone who has made such an admission. What do you say? "Yeah, it sure was." Or lie like a porch dog and say, "I've seen stupider." I just walked off and went fishing.

I have had many horrifying experiences with snakes over the years, and I have lived many, many years, so I will probably write about them again. Next time though, I'll try to come up with a better title.

# 32.

# AN OUTDOORSMEN GUIDE TO POLITICAL CORRECTNESS

In today's politically correct charged and challenged social atmosphere, the very title of this article is incorrect and may bring its adherents screaming and screeching from their parent's basements in protest. Their abject fear of any word that could be remotely defined as sexist would require that "outdoorsman" be changed to "outdoorsperson." Welcome to the weird world of P.C.

Likewise, the word "fisherman" must go into the dustbin of history (or is it peoplestory?). Personally, I just couldn't wrap my head around "fisherpeople." It sounds too much like a manufactured kid's toy. We won't have to worry about the likes of "skeet shooter" though. Unless they come up with "shooteress." However, such made up names are not likely. Before they succeeded in mainstreaming the term "letter carrier" into widespread use, I got into trouble.

I had ordered a book on antique lures and was beginning to think I was going to be too antique to read it by the time it was delivered. When the postal employee named Doris, instead of our regular guy Jim, brought it to the door, in my excitement, I yelled to my wife, "The femailman is here." She handed me the book and slapped me. P.C.ers are very sensitive. It's funny (or not) that the P.C. crowd disputes the very existence of differences in male and female, yet if you don't believe in man-made, catastrophic global warming, you are a "science denier." Strange.

Speaking of which, P.C. people have totally, like totally for sure, embraced global warming. They had to quit calling it that though when the earth's mean temperature didn't deviate for 20 years, and the polar bear population grew exponentially. No problem, they just turned to semantics to bail themselves out. They started calling it "Climate Change." That term is so, I don't know, non-specific and inclusive as to be impossible to disprove, especially since it has been going on since the creation of the earth. And it lends itself to a foolproof caveat I think we sportspeople should adopt.

See, the term precludes them from ever being wrong. It's sort of like the rain percentages the weather forecasters have come up with. If they predict only a 10% chance of showers and it rains, they say "See?" And if they predict 90% and it doesn't, they say "See?" The P.C. people use Climate Change the same way. If there is an absence of tornadoes one year, they blame it on Climate Change. If there is an abundance of tornadoes the next year, Climate Change. See how that works. We've got to get in on this guys! Never again will we have to come up with excuses for our shortcomings and failures.

"Catch anything today, Joe?" "Nah, the bass are bedding" or "Nah, water was too high" or "Nah, my cheap ass depth finder quit working again." Now we can simply say, "Nah, Climate Change," and nobody can dispute it. Accepting and espousing this crap will significantly decrease our capacity for embarrassing ourselves with stupid pretenses. Thanks, P.C. people!

"Cultural Appropriation" is another element P.C. proponents have conjured up and with which we sportspeople have to contend. Generally, it means no one can borrow anything from another country or civilization that did not originate in their own. For instance, it is against P.C. law for Ducky's nephew to dress up as a ninja warrior for Halloween. On my Grandmother's sweet old country soul, I am not kidding.

Fortunately, there are not many situations in which that will affect us. Perhaps if you are caught fishing in the Gulf wearing a sombrero or eating a cold slice of Italian pizza in a deer stand, you might be attacked by a group of wild-eyed, pitch-fork wielding Yale graduates. But it's not likely. A close cousin of "Cultural Appropriation" is "Identity Politics." It is meant, as far as I can figure, to categorize people and things (and possibly animals, vegetables and minerals) into separate groups for some purpose which this old boy cannot comprehend and I doubt they can either. Now, they already detest anyone who fishes, hunts or spends time outdoors. If you do not confine yourself to a coffee shop or a darkened room playing computer—games, you are already labeled an infidel.

What if they take this "Identity Politics" to the next level and go into demonic consultation around a black cauldron in the bowels of some government basement with politicians of their own ilk? And what if said politicos pass some law preventing us from taking fish or game or using implements or strategies not indigenous to our state? You laugh (or not), but it could happen. If it does and you live in Alabama for instance, you would never be able to fish for Kentucky bass or use a Carolina rig or dress your deer with an Arkansas toothpick (I will draw the line at Tennessee whiskey). I know it sounds far-fetched but remember these are the same people who think it's O.K. for men to use women's restrooms.

And remember, you must avoid at all costs identifying yourself as a sportsman in the presence of a member of the "Save the (insert animal here)" crowd. You know, "Save the Speckled Rock Lizard" or "Save the Blind Cave Fish." These people are not only a few shells short of a full box, but their purpose and aims seem to be at odds. They want to save the Killer Whale, which eats Polar Bears, which they also want to save, which eats the harbor seals, which they also want to save, which eats the salmon, which they also want to save. The Inuit Indians also eat the salmon, but they are not interested in saving them because they are, well, people.

Finally, here is one we may not be able to overcome. The adherents of political correctness insist we refrain from using nouns or adjectives that may be derogatory or demeaning to another's physical appearance, mental abilities or social problems. I know entire groups of us who would not be able to communicate. We would just stand around looking at each other and blinking.

Ducky has several names he calls me that I actually answer to. They usually involve my ancestry, bathroom habits, sexual prowess (or lack thereof) and include the words "fat" and "ignorant" and "ugly." And this is when we are playing nice. It gets worse. The P.C.ers labor under the delusion that if we change the words by which we describe those with problems, their affliction will magically disappear. They think if you don't call a drunk, a drunk, he will become sober. I suppose we should refer to him as a connoisseur of cheap wine.

This means I cannot call my friend Stinkin' Jenkins, Stinkin'. I have to call him odoriferously challenged. And I can't call Ducky bat crap crazy. I have to call him intellectually incapacitated. (Since those two words contain 6 syllables each, he will not understand them anyway.) And I can't call these politically correct people blithering idiots. Oh, wait a minute. Yes I can!

# 33.

# OGS

In the contemporary entertainment industry, OG stands for Original Gangster. Now, I am not personally acquainted with any gangster, original or otherwise. But among sportsmen, outdoorsmen and people who live in the real world, OG stands for Old Guy. There is no set chronology that designates a specific age at which a man becomes an OG. I know guys who are 40 that are really 80. Most of them are actuaries or computer programmers and don't get out a lot. But the majority of us just know when we have reached OG prominence. My friend Ducky Jones is terrified that some folks already place him (and me) into the OG category. So, he has expanded the designation to OOG and OOOG, so he can claim "young senior" status. I asked him what comes after OOOG. He said, "DG."

OG's are well known for their inability to accept new ideas. So, as an OG, I had never bought into this "climate change" stuff. However, in the last few years I have begun to change my mind. The summers have definitely been getting hotter and the winters almost unbearably cold. My wife has another explanation, but it couldn't possibly be true. Also, I wonder why the same scientists who champion "climate change" have made no mention about the "geographic alterations," which I find so obvious. Hills that I used to walk up without a deep breath have slowly become mountains, requiring lots of gasping and rest stops. Probably has something to do with the heretofore unnoticed volcanic calderas expanding beneath our feet, like the one in Yellowstone.

By the way, if that one goes off, we won't have to worry about "climate change" anymore. And I'm really concerned they haven't warned us about whatever astronomical or atmospheric anomaly that has caused the recent time differential. Five a.m. gets here earlier and earlier with each passing year. What's up with that? But I digress. And that's O.K. Digression is a common malady among OG's.

The point I was trying to get to is that it is mutually beneficial for those hunters and fishermen who are not considered OG's (known as YG's) to partner with the OG's. It's good for the YG because he can get information he would otherwise not be privy to. For instance, before an outing, an OG can flex his fingers and tell you whether it is going to rain or snow. A really good OG (OOG) can tell you how much precipitation is going to fall within one-tenth of an inch. I defy you to find a TV weatherman who can do that.

The pairing is good for the OG as well because we occasionally require physical assistance. For instance, we may need a little help getting in and out of the boat. That doesn't sound very important, but you have to consider an OG can drown in a foot of water in less than 5 seconds. But the OG knows honey holes in that lake that the YG's generation has never even heard of. And the OG may have to get the YG to loosen the cap on his coffee thermos, but he will later whisper that you should hold your fire on the 4 pointer because, though neither of you can see him, there is an 8 pointer standing in the woods about 20 yards behind. Mutually beneficial.

If you are a YG going camping, an OG is invaluable. Camping requires prodigious planning, and no one can plan better than an OG. Before we sit in our easy chair, we must systematically note and meticulously gather everything we need and envision all unforeseen scenarios. Chewing tobacco, spit cup, TV guide, eyeglasses, TV remote, cold drink, extra cold drink, handkerchief, telephone, hearing aid, dog by footstool (in case you forget to turn hearing aid on and phone rings), and back scratcher. Go to bathroom, lock the back door, and make sure the coffee pot is turned off. All of this must be done before we sit down because it hurts so bad when we get back up. The OG is the perfect guy to prevent leaving on a camping trip without everything you need. Especially toilet paper.

OG's can have loads of fun with a YG. If the lad casts to the deep end of a submerged pine log with a crank bait and gets hung up, the OG can say, "Told ya." And the YG thinks he had been duly warned, and he just didn't hear. After all, the venerable old sage simply exudes trust and would never lie to him. And the YG thinks, "This guy really knows his stuff."

And if the YG makes the same cast and hangs and lands a 6 pounder, the OG can still say, "Told ya" and the YG will think the same thing. It's priceless.

Eyesight, or lack thereof, is usually a problem for all OG's, so we have to be creative in interacting with YG's. After I shoot at a dove or a quail or a duck, I wait to see if the YG says, "Nice shot." If he doesn't, I say, "Didn't lead him enough" Sometimes though, depending on what the YG says can be confusing. With no other references, if you are casting from a small aluminum jon boat and the YG blurts out "Damn!," you don't know if you've hooked him in the back of the head, accidently kicked out the drain plug or passed gas. It can be disconcerting.

Like good eyesight, an OG, as noted earlier, with good hearing is as rare as an honest lawyer. YG's have to take this into consideration when dealing with those of advanced years. A while back my grandson came to me with this confused look on his face and said, "Grampa, I asked Mr. Ducky to help me sight in my new gun and he told me he didn't want a hot dog." As an experienced geezer, I could interpret the misunderstanding easily, but I just told the boy "He's very, very old son. And not too bright. Pay him no attention. I'll help you."

For you YG's thinking about adopting an OG as a partner, there are some other things you might want to know. Occasionally, we have the bladder control of a frightened poodle. We tell the same jokes over and over again. And we are about as fast as a tree sloth. On the other hand, we will usually pay for the beer, we can tell the weight of a bass without a scale, we know how to talk to game wardens and we always, always bring extra napkins to the barbeque. And even an Original Gangster knows you can never have too many napkins at the barbeque.

# 34.

# THE PRICE WAS RIGHT

Ducky and I were rained out of a fishing trip last week and sat on my front porch talking, as we are wont to do since staring at each other is boring. And a little scary. He complained that he had just spent a dollar for free air at the gas station. I said, "Ducky, air hasn't been free for years." He said, "I did not know that. I must have good tires." Hence commenced a conversation about the cost of things and how they have changed over the years.

Now, the first President Ducky and I remember was Eisenhower. If the first one you remember is the second Bush or Obama, go play with your cell phone, because you are neither going to comprehend nor appreciate the information contained herein. If you recollect most of this stuff, you are old. Sorry, but someone had to tell you.

Since we were sipping on one, mixed with Kentucky's finest, Ducky asked, "Remember when coke was a nickel?" "Indeed, I do," I replied. Now, the word "Coke" has to be defined and modified with an explanation. It was (is) a generic term in the South. In Yankeeland and the West, they called it Pop or Soda. In the South, those two words applied to a male relative or a baking additive with which we often brushed our teeth.

And "down hyar," "Coke" was any carbonated beverage. When you ordered one, you were asked to specify "What kind?" Likely as not, you would answer "Nehi orange" or "Pepsi" or "Grapico." I know, I know, it was strange. Milky Ways and Paydays were also five cents. And they were the size of a baby's arm. A kid could survive 3 days on some flavor of coke and a candy bar. For a dime.

"At that station where you got your free air for a dollar Ducky, how much was gas?" He replied, "Too much point 9 cents. 'Member gas wars?" Many moons ago, "gas stations" were "service stations" because, well, they provided service. They not only pumped your gas, but cleaned your windshield and headlights, checked your oil, put "free" air in your tires and took a whisk broom to your front seat. These places were owned by individuals and not corporations. And if two individuals were across the road from one another, they sometimes became more competitive than rutting bucks.

If gas were 30 cents a gallon, one would drop his price a penny and the other would go a penny under that and so on until it got down to 20 cents or so. Now, it was 30 miles to our favorite farm pond, alliteratively named "Pirtle's Puddle," where, according to Farmer Pirtle's poetic sign by the road, "Piddling was Perfect at." My old Plymouth Savoy got 20 mpg, so gas for a round-trip cost about 60 cents. It is a proven scientific fact that teenagers back then would only spend what they needed at a given moment, If you needed 3 gallons of gas, you didn't buy 4. So it cost 50 cents to fish Mr. Pirtle's pond and if you were fishing with artificials and didn't buy live bait, but got gas, a "Coke" and a giant candy bar, the whole trip would set you back $1.20.

When I pointed that number out to Ducky, he concurred and added, "That is about the amount of tax on a balsa wood crankbait today." I added, "And the total price of a True Temper Crippled Shad crankbait back then." Ducky interjected, "Yeah, but my favorite cranker was much more expensive. The Vivif!" "The what?" "Vivif," he repeated. As if he were talking to a three-year-old. "I don't remember that one." "Of course you don't. Your cognitive abilities have been impaired by age and brown whiskey. Either that, or you couldn't afford one. They were over two dollars, you know," he finished in a tone and manner of a land baron addressing a serf.

"Well, how the hell did you afford it?" "Couldn't. I found mine. Only used it on one trip before I lost it to a sunken log. It had a hard rubber body with a double hook in the belly and a flexible tail that actually swam. The most lifelike action I had ever seen. Vivif means "life-like, you know." I asked, "What is that, French?" He said, "Oui." "I didn't know you spoke French." He repeated, "Oui." "You speak any other languages I don't know about?" Ducky said, "Si." I was about to ask him if he spoke Russian, but if he had said "Da," I would, under the sanctions listed in The Great Book of Redneck Rules, have been required to slap him severely about the head and shoulders, so I went back to the subject of lures.

I reminded Ducky that the original Rapala was right expensive too because it was imported. Upwards of a buck seventy-five if indeed birthdays and hard liquor haven't clouded my memory too badly. And people drew conclusions about one's level of sophistication based upon one's pronunciation of that particular name. (Social class recognition has been around a long, long time) If you pronounced it "Rap'ala, you were either a kid or a hillbilly. If you said "Rapa'la, you might get an invitation to an afternoon tea.

Anyway, most crankbaits ran about a dollar and a quarter. The Hula Dancer, Pikie, River Runt, Bomber and the like were popular. The Flatfish, on the other hand, was about half that price and therefore what Ducky and I used if the situation called for such. I got a knockoff version in a box of cereal once. That one only weighed about 1/52nd of an ounce, so you could only cast it about 8 feet (with the wind). But I used it, because "free" is the best price you can get.

The price of topwaters were equivalent to the crankbaits. Around $1.10-$1.50 compared to the five and six bucks today. But their names were so much more intriguing. Dying Flutter, Jitterbug, Torpedo, Crazy Crawler, Lucky 13. Some of these are still around, but in a smaller version. Way back when, most of them were the size of the bass they caught. Bass were not very smart in the old days. One of my favorites was the Bass 'n Bug. It was a bass finish popper with a length of wire connecting a hookless trout fly to the eye of the lure, looking like a tiny bass chasing a bug. I never caught a fish on it, but it looked so real, I couldn't quit using it. Bass were not the only things that weren't very smart in the old days.

Ducky asked me what my "mostest favoritist" lure was back then. "You know very well. The silver spoon." He grinned. He was with me when I caught my first lunker on it. Seven pounds. She pulled the little pram we were in around twice before we got her in the boat. I don't think I changed lures for two years after that. Twenty-five cents. The same price as the three national outdoor magazines and 8 times less than they are today.

The Hawaiian Wiggler was the most popular spinnerbait of the days of yore. It was expensive, at least the price of topwaters. But if you needed distance, that was your lure. You could take your line down to the metal spool of an eight-dollar Bronson baitcaster on a good overhand. If the pond you were fishing were less than two acres, you had to reign in so as not to hit the opposite bank.

The lure we used most, though, was the in-line spinnerbait, specifically the Shyster, not only because they were cheap (50-75 cents) but because they were deadly. White or yellow with black spots, they looked nothing like any known form of aquatic life south of Tennessee, but they caught fish. Any fish. Bass, bluegill, shellcracker, crappie, stumpknockers, even the occasional cat. I think they were named, appropriately, after backwoods Southern lawyers.

You could purchase a dozen pork rinds in a bottle of brine for 30 cents, attach one sliver to a Shyster's treble hook and it was irresistible. Today, of course, we use plastic trailers. Both have their drawbacks. The plastics tear off, rather easily. The pork rind wouldn't tear off if you took a pair of pliers to it. However, if you forgot to remove it through the designated slit after the trip and return it to its bottle of salt water, it would shrivel and dry to a consistency somewhat equal to that of granite. It wasn't coming off. It was easier to buy a new Shyster.

Surprisingly, live bait was not immune to the ravages of inflation. Used to be you could get crickets, two for a penny. The last cage full I bought; they were three cents apiece. For what used to be the price of a Pirtle's trip, today you get 40 of the little bugs. So, you have to spend at least three bucks nowadays, for no self-respecting breamer would go into a bait shop and ask for less than a hundred. The proprietor would likely shake his head in pity at your lack of confidence.

Evening approached and my conversation with Ducky dwindled like the rain. And he said something, uncharacteristically, almost profound. "You know, it isn't the cost of things that made that era notable." I agreed, but didn't say it out loud. It is the memories that make it priceless.

# 35.

# AN ADVENTURE AT
# THE BAIT SHOP LOUNGE

Last Summer, Ducky Jones and Jake Stinkin' Jenkins and I went catfishing down on the river, ostensibly to try out a new bait Jake had concocted, but in reality just to get out of our respective houses. The wives were busy with baby shower plans for somebody's granddaughter. It may have been mine. Men don't particularly pay attention to that kind of stuff, and we don't like to be around that much progesterone. It might be catching.

We parked at an abandoned barn on an acquaintance's property and walked across a couple of acres of open field to get to our fishing hole. We were halfway there before Ducky noticed Jake had a 38-caliber revolver with a 12-inch barrel strapped to his side. Now, it wasn't unusual for Stinkin' to carry such armament, since he is a practicing and legally licensed proponent of Open Carry. But Ducky remarked that we weren't likely to run into any highwaymen down there. Jake informed him it was loaded with snake shot and that we were, after all, headed to a stretch of the Coosa called "Moccasin Gap."

Ducky said, "You don't need that" and promptly produced a pack of chewing tobacco, from which he removed a wad and stuffed it in his cheek. Still walking, after a long moment or two, he let loose a brown stream of juice that splattered against a fence post 5 feet away and said, "When you hit a moccasin between the eyes with a chaw of Red Man, he'll leave you alone." I said, "Jake, this was a cow pasture last Spring. Don't step in the Ducky."

Jake asked Ducky what he was going to do with that huge 14" fillet knife he had strapped to his belt. Ducky replied, "That's in case the tobacco don't work." Even I had to grin at that one. We got to the river, found a suitable sitting place on a sandbank, and baited up. Jake had outdone himself with his new batch of bait. Thank God, he had stored it in a zip lock bag because the stench was almost unbearable. I didn't ask what the ingredients were because I was afraid I couldn't bring myself to touch it if I knew. He had molded it into little squares about the size of crap die and the name of that game was appropriate to the smell. You had to hold your breath and hold the bait at arm's length just to put it on your hook.

We caught channels and blues and yellows with great regularity. They were smallish and we tossed them all back as we caught them. None met the criteria for Ducky's huge knife. But that was O.K.. This was not a food trip; it was an escape destination. We chatted between catches of course and someone postulated they had never even seen a snake, much less a moccasin, in "Moccasin Gap" and we unanimously declared it to be an inappropriate name. Picking up on the irony, I asked if anyone had ever seen a wildcat on "Panther Branch." No one had. Ducky asked, "Has anybody ever seen a Native American on "Indian Camp Road?" We all agreed "No" and we came to the conclusion that most of the names around us were inexplicable, misleading and wrong. So went our chat. Left to random progression, an all-male conversation can devolve quickly. We eventually agree that we all had seen at one time or another, Easy Elaine at the local Pancake House after 1:00 am on Saturday night.

Catfishing and conversation can create dehydration, so as the sun got low, we donated what was left of Stinkin's bait to the river gods, washed our hands as best we could and left for Jenkin's car, discussing where we might stop to quench our thirst on the way home. Since he was driving, he suggested the Bait Shop Lounge, arguing that it had a preemptive name to end a fishing trip. Ducky and I had never heard of it and Jenkins told us it was on the other side of town and on the wrong side of the tracks. We asked how it got its name. He related that many years ago, it was indeed originally a bait shop and had a license to sell off-premises beer, but it failed to prosper and went out of business. It was sold to a less than reputable out-of-town individual with a crooked nose and a matching demeanor and reputation. He quickly dumped the fishing tackle and stock, refurbished and enlarged the interior, kept the license and turned it into a bar.

In order to keep his status as a regular commercial business, he thumbtacked a pack of hooks and a pack of bobbers on the wall but sold beer and liquor on premises with the blessings of an equally corrupt city licensing agent. Jake said a customer once tried to buy the hooks and corks and was severely beaten up and no one ever asked again. Ducky and I laughed. By the time this story was related, Jake had parked in front of the Bait Shop Lounge. It looked like you would expect. The parking lot was unlit. The name of the place was hand-painted on raw plywood leaning up against the building. The parking lot was full of ratty pick-ups and some ominous looking Harleys. There were two very large angry looking dogs chained to a post near the front door. This was not a place you would want to bring a first date.

Ducky and I hesitated to even get out of the car, but Jake was adamant, so we walked across the parking lot like a couple of kids who had been double dog dared. I asked Jake if it was O.K. to open carry in there and he replied, "Nobody's ever said anything." I asked, "You ever wonder why?" Jake grinned and then said, puzzled, "But you know, I've noticed I can't trust anyone to be honest when I'm wearing this thing. When I talk to strangers, they are way too compatible." He went on to explain that if he asked someone he had never met what their favorite color was or some such innocuous question, they would always ask in return, "What's yours?" When he told them, they would say, "Mine too!" I asked again, "You ever wonder why?"

When we walked in, we were greeted by some rather loud, disagreeable "music" with indecipherable lyrics. We old folks think music died when the Eagles broke up. There was a chick (I think) leaning on a pool table staring at us. I told Ducky she needed a face removal. He replied, "You mean a face lift." "No, I don't." I looked around. You just knew there was no toilet paper in the restroom, not that I would ever go in there. But there was no sawdust or brass spittoons on the floor. And the bar didn't have foot rails for standing customers only. There were actually swivel bar stools, of which we appropriated three down on one end and each of us ordered a cold one. Before we had even had a chance to take a sip, this twenty-something year old biker type, trying to grow a goatee and wearing a vest festooned with patches and arms festooned with tattoos, came swaggering by, stopped immediately behind us, and said, in a too loud voice, "Geez, who stinks?" (The entire contents of the Coosa could not have eliminated that odor.)

He looked straight at Jake, who swung around slightly on his stool to show the .38 hogleg strapped to his thigh and said, "Son, I'm sorry. You have obviously mistaken me for someone who gives a rat's rear what you want to know." The guy's eyes enlarged noticeably, and he immediately turned his gaze to Ducky, who was less physically intimidating and wearing, as was his custom, a Gilligan hat covered with trout flies. Now, Ducky has never fished for nor caught a trout in his life, living as he does in the Deep South. It's just his strange style. But it does make him look a little, shall we say, fragile and unassertive. The kid growled, "Is it you?" and wrinkled his nose.

Ducky swiveled his seat all the way around to face his antagonist and said, without a flinch, "Boy, I am the most dangerous man in the state of Alabama. I am too old to fist fight, too proud to run and the only thing left to do is slice and dice." With that, he rested his forearm on the handle of his huge, belted knife. I had not turned around, but I could actually hear the guy swallow. He was not as dumb as I thought, and he was not as intimidating as he thought, and it was beginning to dawn on him. I was the last in line, so he turned his wrath to me. Without looking, I could feel his (rapidly weakening) withering stare on the back of my neck. Now, the only thing I had hanging on my belt was a roll of belly fat. But Ducky said, "Don't even think about it, boy. He's the crazy one." Taking his cue, I affected a twitch in my left eye and turned my head ever so slowly and just stared at him for a moment. I never said a word. He dropped his eyes, muttered an expletive under his breath and just walked away, knowing he had been bested by three old men.

We sat and nursed our beers and giggled for a while. When we finished, Jake signaled the barkeep we were paying up. He sauntered over and said, "You guys are crazy. Didn't you see the motorcycle gang patch on that guy? Are you blind?" I said, "On a good night, we can see all the way to the moon." He grinned and said, "Beer's on the house." As we made our way out, I glanced up over the door. There, thumbtacked over the frame, was a pack of #6 bream hooks and a two-pack of little red and white bobbers. I'll be damned.

Jake dropped me off first. None of us knew where the baby shower was going to be held, but the mystery was solved when I saw twenty cars parked in front of my house. Ducky and Jake said, simultaneously, "Sorry Dude," but they were both grinning ear to ear. I bade them goodbye, walked in my front door, into my living room and my wife walked up, took one whiff and told me to get out of her house. Dejected, on the way to the back yard, I grabbed a half dozen of those little triangular sandwiches off of a tray and stopped by the fridge for my second beer of the night.

I settled into my lawn chair and realized I had been kicked out of my own house by a bunch of chittering and squealing women. But I reviewed the day. I had successfully fished a wild stretch of river, faced down a thug in a seedy bar, got a free beer and shared a few laughs with my rugged outdoor companions. I decided I was, after all, a man's man. I also decided I would never set foot in the Bait Shop Lounge again.

# ABOUT THE AUTHOR

**GARRY BOWERS**, born in Montgomery, Alabama, in 1946, passed away after completing the book in hand. Shotwell is proud to publish this posthumous work. We have previously published Bowers's books *Dixie Days: Reminiscences of a Southern Boyhood* and *Slavery and the Civil War—What Your History Teacher Didn't Tell You.*

A lifelong Alabamian, Bowers had degrees from Troy University, Auburn University, and the University of Alabama. He worked for 20 years as a public-school teacher and administrator and then worked as a deputy sheriff. He served in the Alabama National Guard. All the while he wrote columns for newspapers about hunting and fishing and other subjects.

Mr. Bowers wanted to thank Mark Bowers for assistance with this book.

# BEST SELLERS AND NEW RELEASES

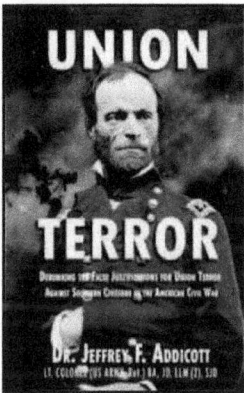

## OVER 90 TITLES FOR YOU TO ENJOY

# SHOTWELLPUBLISHING.COM

**JEFFERY ADDICOTT**
Union Terror: Debunking the
False Justifications for Union Terror

Trampling Union Terror:
Riders of the Second Alabama Cavalry

**MARK ATKINS**
Women in Combat: Feminism Goes to War

**JOYCE BENNETT**
Maryland, My Maryland:
The Cultural Cleansing of a Small Southern State

**GARRY BOWERS**
Slavery and The Civil War:
What Your History Teacher Didn't Tell You

Dixie Days: Reminiscences Of a Southern Boyhood

**JERRY BREWER**
Dismantling the Republic

**ANDREW P. CALHOUN**
My Own Darling Wife: Letters From A
Confederate Volunteer

**JOHN CHODES**
Segregation: Federal Policy or Racism?

Washington's KKK: The Union League During
Southern Reconstruction

**WALTER BRIAN CISCO**
War Crimes Against Southern Civilians

**DAVID T. CRUM**
Stonewall Jackson: Saved by Providence

**STEPHEN DAVIS**
Confederate Triumph: How the South Won Its
War for Independence 1861-1863
Volume One:1861

**JOHN DEVANNY**
Continuities: The South in a Time of Revolution

Lincoln's Continuing Revolution: Essays of M.E.
Bradford and Thomas H. Landess

**JOSHUA DOGGRELL**
Doxed: The Political Lynching of a Southern Cop

**JAMES C. EDWARDS**
What Really Happened?:
Quantrill's Raid On Lawrence, Kansas

**TED EHMANN**
Boom & Bust In Bone Valley: Florida's
Phosphate Mining History 1886-2021

**JOHN AVERY EMISON**
The Deep State Assassination
of Martin Luther King Jr.

**DON GORDON**
Snowball's Chance: My Kidneys Failed,
My Wife Left Me & My Dog Died...

**JOHN R. GRAHAM**
Constitutional History of Secession

**PAUL C. GRAHAM**
Confederaphobia

When The Yankees Come: Former Carolina
Slaves Remember

Nonsense on Stilts: The Gettysburg Address
& Lincoln's Imaginary Nation

**JOE D. HAINES**
*The Diary of Col. John Henry Stover Funk
of the Stonewall Brigade, 1861-1862*

**CHARLES HAYES**
*The REAL First Thanksgiving*

**V.P. HUGHES**
*Col. John Singleton Mosby: In the News 1862-1916*

**TERRY HULSEY**
*25 Texas Heroes*

*The Constitution of Non-State Government:
Field Guide to Texas Secession*

**JOSEPH JAY**
*Sacred Conviction:
The South's Stand for Biblical Authority*

**JAMES R. KENNEDY**
*Dixie Rising: Rules For Rebels*

*Nullifying Federal and State Gun Control:
A How-To Guide For Gun Owners*

*When Rebel Was Cool:
Growing Up In Dixie, 1950-1965*

*Reconstruction: Destroying the Republic
and Creating an Empire*

**WALTER D. KENNEDY**
*The South's Struggle: America's Hope*

*Lincoln, The Non-Christian President:
Exposing The Myth*

*Lincoln, Marx, and the GOP*

**J.R. & W.D. KENNEDY**
*Jefferson Davis: High Road to Emancipation
and Constitutional Government*

*Yankee Empire:
Aggressive Abroad and Despotic at Home*

*Punished With Poverty: The Suffering South*

*The South Was Right! 3rd Edition*

**LEWIS LIBERMAN**
*Snowflake Buddies; ABC Leftism For Kids!*

**PHILIP LEIGH**
*The Devil's Town: Hot Springs During
The Gangster Era*

*U.S. Grant's Failed Presidency*

*The Causes of the Civil War*

*The Dreadful Frauds: Critical Race Theory
And Identity Politics*

**JACK MARQUARDT**
*Around The World In 80 Years: Confessions
of a Connecticut Confederate*

**MICHAEL MARTIN**
*Southern Grit: Sensing The Siege at Petersburg*

**SAMUEL MITCHAM**
*The Greatest Lynching In American History:
New York, 1863*

*Confederate Patton: Richard Taylor and
The Red River Campaign*

**CHARLES T. PACE**
*Lincoln As He Really Was*

*Southern Independence. Why War? The War
To Prevent Southern Independence*

**JAMES R. ROESCH**
*From Founding Fathers To Fire Eaters*

**KIRKPATRICK SALE**
*Emancipation Hell: The Tragedy Wrought
By Lincoln's Emancipation Proclamation*

**JOSEPH SCOTCHIE**
*The Asheville Connection:
The Making of a Conservative*

*Samuel T. Francis and
Revolution from the Middle*

SHOTWELLPUBLISHING.COM

Green Altar (Literary Imprint)

**CATHARINE SAVAGE BROSMAN**
*An Aesthetic Education
and Other Stories (2nd Ed)*

*Chained Tree, Chained Owls: Poems*

*Aerosols and Other Poems*

*Partial Memoirs*

**RANDALL IVEY**
*A New England Romance:
And Other Southern Stories*

*The Gift of Gab*

**SUZANNE JOHNSON**
*Maxcy Gregg's Sporting Journals 1842-1858*

**JAMES E. KIBLER, JR.**
*Tiller : Claybank County Series, Vol. 4*

*The Gentler Gamester*

*Beyond The Stone: Poems of Tribute
& Remembrance*

**THOMAS MOORE**
*A Fatal Mercy:
The Man Who Lost The Civil War*

**PERRIN LOVETT**
*The Substitute, Tom Ironsides 1*

**KAREN STOKES**
*Belles*

*Carolina Twilight*

*Honor in the Dust*

*The Immortals*

*The Soldier's Ghost: A Tale of Charleston*

**WILLIAM THOMAS**
*Runaway Haley:
An Imagined Family Saga*

*The Field of Justice: Moonshine
and Murder in North Georgia*

**CLYDE N. WILSON**
*Southern Poets and Poems, 1606-1860:
The Land They Loved, Volume 1*

*Confederate Poets and Poems, Vol1
The Land They Loved, Volume II*

Gold-Bug
(Mystery & Suspense Imprint)

**BRANDI PERRY**
*Splintered: A New Orleans Tale*

**MARTIN WILSON**
*To Jekyll and Hide*

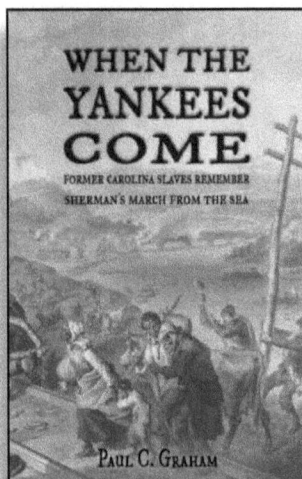

www.ingramcontent.com/pod-product-compliance
Lightning Source LLC
Chambersburg PA
CBHW052046090426
42739CB00010B/2066